D0818891

THE
Dog
Behavior
ANSWER BOOK

Practical Insights & Proven Solutions
for Your Canine Questions

ARDEN MOORE

ILLUSTRATED BY MATT AMBRE

FOREWORD BY JOHN GROGAN

Storey Publishing

*The mission of Storey Publishing is to serve our customers
by publishing practical information that encourages personal
independence in harmony with the environment.*

Edited by Lisa H. Hiley
Art direction by Mary Velgos
Cover design by Kent Lew
Text design by Jessica Armstrong
Text production by Jennifer Jepson Smith
Illustrations © by Matt Ambre
Indexed by Christine R. Lindemer, Boston Road Communications

The information in this book is true and complete to the best of our knowledge. All
recommendations are made without guarantee on the part of the author or Storey Publishing. The author and publisher disclaim any liability in connection with the use of this
information. For additional information please contact Storey Publishing, 210 MASS
MoCA Way, North Adams, MA 01247.

Storey books are available for special premium and promotional uses and for customized editions. For further information, please call 1-800-793-9396.

Printed in China by Regent Publishing Services
10 9 8 7 6 5 4 3 2 1

Library of Congress Cataloging-in-Publication Data

Moore, Arden.
    The dog behavior answer book : practical insights and proven solutions for your
canine questions / by Arden Moore ; Illustrated by Matt Ambre.
        p. cm.
    Includes bibliographical references and index.
    ISBN-13: 978-1-58017-644-6; ISBN-10: 1-58017-644-5 (pbk. : alk. paper)
1. Dogs—Behavior—Miscellanea. 2. Dogs—Training—Miscellanea. I. Title.

SF433.M64 2006
636.7'0835—dc22

                                                    2006020472

DEDICATION

I dedicate this book to my delightful friends Cindy and Flo; my dog-adoring siblings, Deb, Karen, and Kevin; my wonderful niece Chrissy and nephew Andy; my cool dog Chipper; and our favorite canine play pals, Buddy, Cleo, Stella, and Gracie.

CONTENTS

Find out what makes a dog behave like a dog. Learn about canine senses, emotions, and instincts. Discover fascinating facts about dog intelligence, puppy love, and breed-specific behaviors.

Dogs and people have lived together for eons, but we don't always communicate well with our canine companions. Brush up on barking, learn about body language, and sharpen your ability to speak "canine-ese."

Our dogs often have habits that we find puzzling, amusing, and sometimes downright disgusting. Find out more about canine quirks and foibles and learn how to change the ones you can't live with.

FOREWORD

As dog owners, my wife Jenny and I were — I won't mince words here — totally clueless. We picked out a puppy without first researching breeds or their personality traits. We didn't insist on meeting the sire. We went on curb appeal alone, choosing looks over temperament. We ended up falling in love at first sight with an adorable yellow Labrador retriever pup who quickly morphed into a 97-pound steamroller of unbridled energy. We named him Marley and spent the next 13 years trying to get him under control, never quite succeeding.

I, only half jokingly, dubbed Marley the world's worst dog, and in many ways he was. He crashed through screens, dug through drywall, gnawed furniture, swallowed jewelry, stole food off the kitchen table, and rooted through trash. He yanked at his leash and drank from the bathtub. He joyfully lunged at guests, leaping up on them with muddy paws to plant wet kisses on their faces. He sniffed crotches and flung drool through the air. Not even dog lovers appreciated it.

What I now realize is that Marley wasn't the worst dog, only one of the worst trained dogs. Jenny and I ran our house like a democracy, and Marley soon learned he had an equal vote. Obey orders? No way! He never did quite get the whole chain-of-command thing.

That's where Arden Moore's *The Dog Behavior Answer Book* could have helped us in a big way. Had we had Arden's commonsense expertise then, we would have better understood what motivated Marley's bad-boy behavior and been able to formulate a strategy to change, or at least temper, it. Good, solid advice from knowledgeable experts is the first step to having a reliably well-behaved pet who will bring joy and pleasure to its owners, not frustration and heartache.

Then again, had I followed Arden's wise advice in this book, Marley might have been so good I never would have been tempted to write a book about him. No doubt about it, bad dogs make for good reading. But good dogs are what every pet owner wants — and deserves. Arden and her team of animal-behavior experts can show you the way.

— John Grogan
Author of *Marley & Me: Life and Love with the World's Worst Dog*

PREFACE

If only our dogs could get by on their cute looks. After all, many people are initially drawn to a particular puppy or dog because of its physical appearance. "Aren't her floppy ears adorable?" "How can I say no to that sweet face?"

Unfortunately, some dogs grow up to be more challenging than cute, more fearful than fun, more bossy than benign. The people/pet honeymoon ends abruptly and the problem-solving phase begins. Your dog puzzles you. Why does he chase that tennis ball again and again? Or greet your date by sniffing his butt? Or bark-bark-bark whenever you speak on the phone? You want answers to save the remaining leather shoes in your closet, the prize roses in your garden, and the plush carpet in your living room.

You wish you could wave a magic wand and engage in a meaningful person-to-dog chat. You want to know why your dog wants to pick a fight with your dishwasher, but runs with his tail tucked from a kid on a skateboard. You want to learn how to stop her from yanking on the leash and stealing your pillow at bedtime.

That's why I wrote this book. Think of *The Dog Behavior Answer Book* as a guide to how dogs think. What makes this book stand out like a Great Dane in a pack of Yorkies is that I answer actual questions from owners like you who just want enjoy a great relationship with that tail-wagger sharing your home. During the past few years, I've been collecting queries posed to me during appearances on television and radio pet shows, at dog events (my favorite was judging America's Search for the Least Obedient Dog), at public speaking presentations, and as a former pet columnist for *Prevention*. Once people find out what I do for a living, they unleash their questions. *Why does my dog . . .? How can I get my dog to stop . . .? What is the best way to teach my dog to . . .?* I hear from people at dog parks, bookstores, weddings, even public bathrooms.

A friend jokingly calls me Dr. Doo — short for Doctor Doolittle — due to the number of times she has witnessed me walk through solutions with a frustrated dog owner. Of course, I'm not a doctor. I don't even play one on TV. But I am a pet expert who has worked with the very best in the fields of veterinary medicine and companion animal behavior. I'm committed to finding useable truths and to communicating workable solutions to frustrated dog owners.

I invite you to paw through these pages. You might nod in agreement as you read some of these questions from other dog lovers and then sense the light bulb click inside you as I spotlight practical solutions. The legendary Doctor Doolittle could talk to the animals. I'm here to deliver straight talk to you.

Paws Up!

Arden Moore

ACKNOWLEDGMENTS

I wish to thank all the veterinarians, animal behaviorists, dog trainers, animal shelter directors, and dog lovers who generously shared their time, talents, and ideas in this book. Special thanks to canine behavior experts Alice Moon-Fanelli, Patrick Melese, and Pia Silvani, as well as my editor, Lisa Hiley. Together, we can reach out and improve the lives of dogs everywhere.

PART I

The Nature of Being a Dog

Put yourself in your dog's paws

for a moment. Some 15,000 years ago, dogs and humans developed a relationship unparalleled in history. In exchange for food and shelter, dogs have helped humans in countless ways, becoming our partners, coworkers, and pals. Over the centuries, people have redesigned the dog, creating many distinct breeds with a wide range of physical characteristics and behaviors. Some breeds weigh more than one hundred pounds, while others can literally fit in a teacup. Ears can be floppy, pointy, or in-between. Coats come in textures from dangling dreadlocks to the nearly naked.

We have created canines for herding, hunting, guarding, and just lounging on laps. In the process, however, we've taken away what comes naturally to dogs and left them with an identity crisis. We've removed them from the social structure of the pack and eliminated their need to hunt for food. And yet we scold them when they seek outlets for their innate need to dig and chew, especially when our gardens or shoes are at stake. In spite all of our meddling, though, the true nature of dogs never wavers: They love us just the way we are.

Brainy Breeds

Q Certain dog breeds seem to be smarter than others, so I purposely chose a Border collie in part because of the breed's reputation for brains. I didn't want to fuss with a less-intelligent breed when it came to teaching basic obedience. I don't have the patience to keep trying and trying to teach a dog to sit or to stay. So far, I've been really happy with Einstein's response to training, but I'm curious: How can I figure out just how smart he is?

A In the canine classroom, your aptly named Einstein rates as the tail-wagging valedictorian. Other top students include poodles, German shepherds, and golden retrievers. Breeds who might need some after-school tutoring include Afghan hounds, basenjis, and bulldogs. Before owners of these dogs bark at me in protest, please keep in mind that exceptions — both bright and not so bright — exist in every breed.

Sizing up a dog's brainpower can be tricky, because they don't think the way that we do. Dogs are not begging to enroll in the canine version of Mensa or stealing the newspaper to do the crossword puzzle. Because certain breeds were created to excel at certain tasks, your Border collie can run circles around a Japanese chin when it comes to herding sheep because he possesses the genes to shepherd a flock. But I'd put my money on a beagle sniffing out a rabbit faster than a Border collie, since the almighty nose is a bragging right among hound breeds.

But almost any dog can learn a wide variety of obedience cues if taught with patience. Some can acquire an astonishing array of behaviors. Service dogs are an amazing example of the canine brain in action. These highly trained dogs are encouraged to exercise "intelligent disobedience" when confronting a situation that could harm their human charges. A guide dog, for example, knows not to budge forward when facing a hole or other hazard, despite his blind owner's insistence.

Developing a foolproof method of testing canine intelligence remains an ongoing challenge for dog trainers, breeders, and animal behaviorists. One pioneer in this field is Stanley Coren, a renowned Canadian psychologist and exceptional dog trainer. In *The Intelligence of Dogs,* Dr. Coren ranks 133 breeds from smart as a whip to dumb as a brick, pointing out there are variations and exceptions in every breed. He devised a canine IQ test that strives to identify several levels of intelligence: adaptive, obedient, and instinctive.

Breeds ranking in the top 10 smartest can grasp new commands in fewer than five repetitions and obey a known cue the first time it is given 95 percent of the time. The Border collie heads this elite class and is joined by poodles, German shepherds, golden retrievers, Doberman pinschers, Shetland sheepdogs, Labrador retrievers, papillons, Rottweilers, and Australian cattle dogs.

Breeds in the bottom 10 often require up to 100 repetitions to understand a new command and will obey a known cue the first time it is given only 25 percent of the time. Even if they know how to *sit*, they may need to hear the word four or five times before they plop their rear ends down. This list, which is definitely subject to debate, includes the Shih Tzu, basset hound, mastiff, beagle, Pekingese, bloodhound, borzoi, chow chow, bulldog, basenji, and Afghan hound.

Here are a few fun ways to figure out how smart your own dog is.

◆ **THE TOWEL TEST:** When your dog is lying down, drape a large bath towel over his head and time how long it takes for him to lose the towel. Smart dogs master this in less than 15 seconds while slow learners can take more than 30 seconds.

◆ **THE BUCKET TEST:** Line up three buckets (size is not important, but use ones made of lightweight material like plastic). Show your dog his favorite treat or toy and let him watch you place it under one of these upside-down buckets. Divert his attention away from the buckets for a few seconds and then ask him to find the hidden prize. A smart dog makes a beeline to the correct bucket while slower learners may knock over the other two buckets before finally finding the prize under the bucket.

◆ **THE LEASH TEST:** Pick a time that you do not customarily walk your dog — say mid-morning or mid-afternoon. Without saying anything, pick up the leash and your house keys in full view of your dog. A smart dog associates the leash and keys with a walk and becomes excited at the prospect of going out. A not-quite-so-bright dog won't make the connection and may need to hear "Want to go for a walk?" before jumping for joy. (Of course, some more phlegmatic dogs may just not be in the mood for a walk!)

Remember that canine IQ tests have limitations, one of which is that the results are subjective and evaluated by people, not other dogs. So a dog who may seem dumb to us could be the leader of the pack in the eyes of other dogs. Whatever the test results, the important thing is to value the love your dog gives you more than the number of brain cells he maximizes.

Superhuman Senses

Q My Siberian husky can be snoozing upstairs in the back bedroom, but within seconds of a bag of potato chips being opened on the first floor, she suddenly appears, tail wagging and ready to share. When we go out on walks, I am amazed at how she sniffs out a cat hiding under a bush or tracks down the smallest bit of something edible on the ground. She can spot a squirrel scampering up a tree faster than I can but will sometimes stop and stare intently at a stick or a rock as though she expects it to move. When it comes to our senses, how do we compare to dogs?

A We all know better than to challenge our dogs to a hearing contest. Canine ears, whether erect like a German shepherd dog, dropped like a Labrador retriever, or folded like a bloodhound, capture more sounds at greater distances and wider frequencies than human ears. Even breeds like cocker spaniels with thick, floppy ears can distinguish the sound of their owner's car from all other traffic a block or more away, though your husky's pricked ears probably give her an advantage in hearing the crinkle of a chip bag from several rooms away.

> **PAW PRINTS**
> Laika, a Siberian husky mix, was the first dog in space. The Soviets launched her aboard Sputnik II in 1957. Laika is Russian for "bark."

Despite their many different shapes and sizes, canine ears have the same basic function: to zero in on sounds (especially that magic word *treat,* or, in your case, the rustle of a potato chip bag) and to help the dog maintain equilibrium while moving. Ears also play an important role in canine communication and can express happiness, playfulness, curiosity, submissiveness, and dominance, for example.

Hearing prowess, however, takes second place to a dog's acute ability to smell. The phrase "led by the nose" takes on a whole new meaning in the canine world. Olfactory receptor cells inside the canine nose are bolstered by tiny hairs called cilia that are coated with mucous to help trap scents. People have about 5 million olfactory receptor cells compared with more than 100 million in dogs. These receptors are capable of breaking down the individual ingredients in each scent. So not only can your dog tell if you're baking a chicken or a turkey, he can also distinguish the particular spices you put in the stuffing.

CAN YOU HEAR ME?

Hertz (Hz) is a measure of sound frequency or cycles per second. People can hear sounds in a frequency range between 63 and 23,000 Hz. Dogs can hear in ranges between 67 and 45,000 Hz, but they take a back-seat to the family cat in hearing abilities. Cats can capture sounds between 45 and 64,000 Hz, making them much better at tuning in to a mouse in the house.

Bottom line: your dog can smell about a million times better than you can (although he probably smells worse before bath time)! The bigger the dog and the longer the muzzle, the better his ability to smell. A bloodhound, for example, has about 300 million of these cells compared to a dachshund with 125 million.

In the battle of the senses, we compete with dogs most closely in the field of vision. We rely on our eyes more than our dogs do. Canine eyes are much more sensitive to movement and to light than ours, but they can't focus on objects as well as we can.

Dogs also tend to be nearsighted, which explains why your dog can spot a bird flying by at dusk but may fixate on a motionless object that you can clearly see is not a squirrel, or have trouble spotting a bright yellow tennis ball from a foot away. Their large pupils and wide field of vision enables them to zoom in on moving objects or potential prey. Dogs do have better peripheral vision, however. Standing still, dogs can see up to 250 degrees without turning their heads, while humans can see, at best, up to 180 degrees.

In summary, your dog wins by a nose and is all ears, at least compared with you.

Psychic Pooch

Q My three-year-old Australian shepherd must be psychic or a mind reader. Each day before I arrive home, he waits for me in front of the living room window. My kids get home from school before I do and they watch in amusement as Rocco stops playing and heads for his designated spot. Rocco likes everyone in the family, but he is definitely my dog. I don't arrive home at the same time every day, but he is always there waiting. Does he really know when I'm on my way?

A You are blessed with an ESP — Extra Sensory Pooch. The quick answer is that some dogs do seem to possess extrasensory powers, but we have yet to unravel the mysteries behind such canine abilities as sensing an earthquake in advance, finding home from miles away, or alerting a person about to have an epileptic seizure. The topic has attracted scientists from all over the globe, including Dr.

Rupert Sheldrake, former director of studies in biochemistry and cell biology at Cambridge University in England and author of *Dogs That Know When Their Owners Are Coming Home and Other Unexplained Powers of Animals.*

Dr. Sheldrake suggests that the ability of some dogs to accurately anticipate the arrival of their owners depends on a kind of telepathic bond. He calls this his theory of morphic resonance. He has tested his theory with many different dogs and their owners. The story of JT may help explain why Rocco seems to be able to read your mind. JT, a mixed-breed dog, could accurately predict when his owner would return to her home in Manchester, England, and would be waiting for her at the front door. Sheldrake's television crew set up two cameras, one on the owner when she prepared to head home from work and one inside her home. The return trips were entirely at random, made at different times with different modes of transportation, but JT managed to be in position to await his owner's arrival 85 percent of the time.

After collecting data on hundreds of similar situations involving dogs of various breeds and mixes, Dr. Sheldrake could find no link between "owner awareness" and level of intelligence, nor did he find any correlation to breed, age, or level of training. After five years of extensive research involving thousands of people who own and work with animals, however, Sheldrake conclusively proves what many pet owners already know — there is a strong connection between humans and animals that lies beyond present-day scientific understanding.

Whatever the explanation, Rocco clearly views you as his trusted ally and friend. Who needs a clock to tell time when his love for you appears timeless?

Ginny Conquers Her Fears

SEPARATED FROM HER MOTHER at three weeks of age, the Rottweiler puppy spent five weeks in a barn with her littermates. When adopted by Cindy and Grace, the young pup feared people, strange objects, unfamiliar sounds, and sudden movements. Her new owners, who had two older dogs at home, wanted to help Ginny develop social skills and confidence. They knew that they had to take their time introducing Ginny to new sights and sounds. Rushing her into new experiences could backfire and cause her to develop full-blown phobias.

They started by spending hours quietly sitting with Ginny on their front porch. Each time a car, person, or dog passed by, they would hand her wonderful treats. Eventually, she stopped cowering in the corner and began to nibble the treats. Once she appeared calm and relaxed on the porch, they took Ginny for walks with their older dogs flanking her sides.

With objects that frightened the puppy, the women played a canine version of Hansel and Gretel. For example, Ginny was afraid of garbage cans, so they repeatedly placed a trail of small treats leading up to one. At first, Ginny would only cautiously take the farthest treats but she eventually grew brave enough to eat the ones near the can. In time she realized that garbage cans would not harm her.

Ginny did beautifully with the other dogs in my puppy class, but was extremely fearful of people. To socialize the pups and teach them to trust people, we play "pass the puppy," a game where each puppy is handed around the circle of owners to be petted and talked to. This game would have been too traumatic for Ginny, so we treated her differently. Whenever she mustered enough confidence to approach people on her own, they tossed a treat on the floor without making eye contact or trying to touch her. Soon she began coming closer to people in the class.

For the next stage, the class sat in chairs and extended their open hands containing treats to Ginny without making eye contact or bending toward her. We added the cue "say hi" when she touched her nose to their palm. Ginny gradually learned that even standing people, who look more threatening, are friendly.

We worked with Ginny through four levels of training. While still cautious in new situations, she now deals with the world with more confidence. When their older dogs died, Cindy and Grace adopted another puppy, and it was great to see Ginny take over the role of canine teacher with her new friend. This lovely dog serves as a great example of how careful, patient training can help a young pup conquer her fears.

Contributed by Pia Silvani, CPDT

True Puppy Love

Q I adore my dog and would do anything to keep her safe and happy. I love to spoil her with new toys and take her with me in the car. She wags her tail at me, gives me sloppy kisses, and rushes to greet me when I come home. I know that I truly love her, but are dogs capable of loving us back in the same way that we love them?

A For thousands of years, "love" wasn't a concept that people thought of in connection with dogs. The initial relationships between early humans and wild canines most likely developed around a mutual need for food and an ability to help each other hunt. Dogs were more like work partners than dearly cherished family members. But over the centuries, as the role of the dog evolved beyond a strictly business relationship, people began to become more emotionally attached to their canine companions.

Particularly within the past two decades, dogs have rapidly moved from being backyard protectors to bedroom-blanket stealers. We speak glowingly of how our dogs race to our front doors and greet us with smiling faces, swishing tails, and wiggling hips. We brag that our dogs comfort us when we feel blue and stay by our bedside when we are ill. Are these acts of loyalty and devotion, or simply servitude and respect? Do our dogs rush to greet us because they are truly delighted by our return or because they need to go outside or want food? Do they remain by our side when we're sick because they truly care, or are they regarding us as members of their pack and acting out of a protective instinct?

In short, do dogs actually feel love and can they express this powerful emotion? While humans have conquered polio, landed astronauts on the moon, and created voice-activated computers, we have yet to come up with a scientific test to support or dispute the notion that dogs truly love us. I posed this question to a few experts in the field, however, and I bet their answers will agree with what most dog owners believe to be true.

Marty Becker, one of America's best-known veterinarians and author of *The Healing Power of Pets,* says that dogs "truly love unconditionally. I think a dog's love is greater than human love. Dogs don't judge anyone. If you're bald or overweight, it doesn't matter to a dog. Their sense of loyalty is tremendous."

According to Bernie Rollin, professor of philosophy at Colorado State University in Fort Collins, "If anybody loves us, certainly our dogs do. Despite the lack of a common language, dogs are capable of conveying love to us. These days, in the face of alienation and cynicism and with three out of five marriages ending in divorce, pets provide us a safe place to give and receive love in the face of this crazy society. Perhaps the better question to ask is, how many people leave their dogs versus how many dogs leave their people?"

And finally, from Alan Beck, professor at Purdue University and author of *Between Pets and People: The Importance of Animal Companionship:* "How do you measure dogs' love when we don't even understand the basis of human love beyond biology? If a dog is really dedicated to you because you are a source of food and comfort, does that really cheapen its love? I don't think so. I think dogs feel dog love. Unfortunately, there are no objective tests. It will be a long time before we truly understand what's going on between dogs and people."

Until the language barrier between our two species lifts, a definitive answer remains unknown. But for now, I'm casting my vote with the viewpoint that we are doggone lucky to be loved by our canine companions.

The Dog as Psychiatrist

Q Last year was a tough one for me. My mother died, I divorced, and I moved to a new state with a new job. There have been lots of tears and days of depression, but my loving papillon, Ginger, has been right by my side the whole time. When I talk to her about my problems, she sits very attentively and will even gently touch my arm with her paw. Each time, I find myself feeling a little bit better. Can dogs read our moods and help us deal with emotional heartache?

A Ginger, your furry therapist, definitely taps into your moods. Like other dogs, she has learned that you tend to be most affectionate when you are happy or sad. Since the days when Sigmund Freud, the father of psychoanalysis, emphasized the therapeutic value that dogs offer to people, mental health experts have recognized that dogs can play a vital role in comforting and encouraging those who are suffering.

Our dogs often seem to be able to shoo away the blues, turn sadness into gladness, and restore self-confidence. They do seem to care about our moods. They calm us down. They listen without interruption or judgment, just like a psychologist.

Dogs make great therapists because they provide unconditional empathy, positive regard, and genuineness. They are great listeners who don't judge. They allow us to talk out a problem and to let off some steam, which reduces our distress and lowers our blood pressure. This unqualified acceptance allows dogs to touch all types of people, from those experiencing mental or physical illnesses to those who live alone or who need motivation to leave the house and get some exercise.

Ginger has plenty of canine company. Throughout history, dogs have served as confidants and emotional support systems for many people, including the famous and infamous. When Mary Queen of Scots was imprisoned in the Castle of Fotheringhay in England, she was denied human contact except for a priest and a servant woman, but she was permitted to keep her terrier, Geddon. As she approached the gallows to be beheaded, Mary hid her dog under her long skirt because she wanted him to be with her to the very end.

During World War II, General Dwight D. Eisenhower took Caicca, his Scottish terrier, with him during his North Africa tour. In letters to his wife Mamie, Eisenhower remarked that Caicca was the only companion he could really talk to and the only one who would not turn the conversation back to the topic of war.

For everyday problems, nothing beats a canine pal. I know that when I return home feeling drained or depressed, my mood quickly lifts when Chipper greets me with a full-body wiggle, clutching her favorite toy in her mouth and wagging her tail.

Solution for Serious Shyness

Q We recently rescued an extremely shy greyhound named Cyrus from a farm where he was kept in a barn for nearly the first year of his life. He and a bunch of other greyhounds were virtually isolated from the rest of the world and left to starve by an uncaring breeder. Cyrus acts anxious and submissive, and often cowers or slinks away when we try to pet him. He is afraid of everyday sights and sounds like vacuum cleaners and televisions. What can we do to boost his confidence and conquer his shyness?

A Cyrus has a lot to process after his many months inside a very small world. He is still transitioning from those bad puppy days and has yet to realize that your home is both loving and permanent. It is important that you exercise lots of gentleness and patience with him while he adjusts to his new life. When I adopted Chipper, she was just over a year old and had lived in three shelters and one husky rescue camp. Like Cyrus, she lacked exposure to items and activities most dogs take for granted. She paced nervously inside my house. On her leash, she would walk side to side, seeming to be on the lookout for a place to hide. If I spoke loudly, she would go belly-up and cower. It took about six months of consistent obedience training and consistent daily routines for Chipper's true personality to begin to flourish. These days she is a happy, confident jokester, always ready for a car ride and eager to make new friends.

The same transformation can happen with Cyrus. Time is your ally as you and your family strive to earn Cyrus's trust. It is common for submissive dogs to cower, avoid direct eye contact, and try to make themselves look smaller to avoid conflict. In extreme situations, they will tuck their tail between their legs and expose their bellies. In dog language, these actions convey that the dog poses no challenge to you — whom he regards as higher in the hierarchy.

Cyrus will gain confidence if he learns the household rules with plenty of TLC and support. Start by not forcing him into any scary situations. Try to move slowly around him and let him know that he can trust you to act consistently. Establish a routine for him and stick to it. Create a safe place for him in a corner or provide him with a crate where he can retreat with his back to a wall. If he musters the courage to come to you when you are sitting still, don't leap to reach out and touch him. Let him make the first moves for now. Slowly extend your hand for him to sniff before accepting a gentle pet from you. Avoid patting the top of his head, as your hand over him might feel like a threat. Your tone of voice is vital. Always use soft, upbeat, or warm tones. Never yell or speak harshly because you will only instill more fear.

Mealtime offers a special opportunity to shoo away Cyrus's shyness and bolster the bond between you. Hand-feed him his meals and treats. You may need to start one piece at a time. If he backpedals, remain still until he returns to you. If he acts too scared, toss the treats a little bit away from you and resume hand-feeding when he regains some confidence.

Regular exercise will not only help Cyrus relax but will further develop your relationship. At first, stick to short walks around your immediate neighborhood. These outings allow Cyrus to build up a database of familiar sights, sounds, and smells. If a car backfiring or other noise causes him to try to bolt, move him along quickly to distract him and give him the chance to settle down. Speak in a happy, confident tone while continuing your walk.

Inside your home or fenced backyard, engage Cyrus in some confidence-building activities like teaching him a trick and offering a food reward and plenty of praise. Don't make a big deal about appliances like the vacuum or dishwasher that may frighten him. If you treat them matter-of-factly, he will learn that they pose no threat. With consistently kind and gentle treatment, most shy dogs warm up and trust their immediate family members within a matter of weeks, and you should begin to see Cyrus's true personality emerge.

Once this occurs, I recommend you enroll Cyrus in a basic dog obedience class so he can have the chance to be around other dogs in a controlled setting. At this stage, you can work also on conquering Cyrus's shyness around newcomers to the house and strangers he meets when he is out and about with you. Ask your friends who visit not to make direct eye contact with Cyrus and to sit quietly. As Cyrus's curiosity takes hold, have your friends offer him treats so he will form a positive association with visitors. Take things slowly and let Cyrus show you when he is ready to move on to the next stage of becoming a confident, happy dog.

Preparing for Puppy Pandemonium

Q My husband and I are adopting a 10-week-old puppy. We want to make sure that our home is safe for him and from him! We have nice antiques and expensive rugs that we don't want chewed up or knocked over. Plus, we worry that the puppy could swallow something that could hurt him. How can we best prepare our home for our new family member?

A You are wise to puppy proof your house now, before your new family member comes home. Puppies are energetic and curious. In their first few months of life, one of the main ways they investigate is by taste testing their surroundings. They demonstrate a real knack for getting into trouble and can quickly destroy household items and swallow things they shouldn't before you know it.

Start preparing your home for your bundle of joy by getting down on his level — literally. Sit down on the floor of each room where your puppy will be permitted to roam and look around for potential hazards that might be within his reach. These include electrical and telephone cords, houseplants on or near the floor, window shade and curtain drawstrings, throw rugs, trashcans or storage containers, and anything else that is on or near the floor that is small enough to fit into a puppy's mouth or light enough to be knocked over. Think about materials such as wicker and cardboard that might not seem tempting to you but may attract a teething pup. Loose belongings such as shoes, toys, books and magazines, and other items will be fair game at first, so form the habit of picking up clutter from the floors. (Having a puppy around can be good incentive for messy children to put away their belongings!)

If you plan to give your puppy access to your kitchen or a bathroom, make sure cabinet doors near the floor are securely fastened. As a further precaution, consider storing all cleaning products and other toxic items in a higher location for now. A hanging shower curtain won't survive a puppy attack. Make sure it's tucked inside the tub if your pup spends time in the bathroom alone.

Puppies can find trouble just about anywhere, so at first, limit your pup's access to just two or three rooms of the house. The fewer rooms your puppy is allowed to visit, the less puppy proofing you'll have to do. Once he grows out of the chewing stage, and is reliably housebroken, you can gradually give him the run of the house. He has earned it! By the way, many dogs happily learn to relax in a single room (kitchen, basement, family room, for example) when the family is away, even though they are used to roaming around the rest of the time. You'll have a deeper and more satisfying relationship, however, with a dog who knows how to behave no matter where he is in the house, so don't rely on restricting his access as a permanent solution.

After checking the inside of your home for potential problems, step outdoors and review your backyard with your puppy in mind. Again, get down on his level by crouching down and checking out the view. Look for objects that your puppy can chew on and swallow, such as garden tools, children's toys, and other small objects. Pay close attention to your fencing to make certain there are no broken areas or gaps where your puppy could escape.

Puppies love to gnaw, and garden plants can be a tempting treat to a youngster exploring his world with his mouth. Take a look at the plant species in your yard and find out if any of them are poisonous to dogs. I recommend the American Society for the Prevention of Cruelty to Animals (ASPCA) Animal Poison Control Center's Web site (www.aspca.org) for a list of dog-friendly and dog-dangerous plants. Any plant that is potentially toxic should be removed or blocked off with secure fencing, such as chicken wire.

Remember, too, that a rambunctious puppy can dig up a garden before you know what he's up to. If you have areas of soft dirt or sand in your yard, cover them by spreading out some chicken wire weighed down with large rocks to discourage the pup from digging. Digging is a difficult habit to break, so it's best to keep it from starting in the first place. Otherwise, your beautiful garden could end up looking like the surface of the moon.

For your puppy's safety, dispose of any pesticides or chemical fertilizers you might be using in your garden and switch to safer, more natural methods of pest control and plant feeding. Be particularly aware of poisonous bait designed to kill snails and slugs, as this can be very appealing to dogs, and very deadly. If your puppy will be allowed to keep you company while you are in your garage, pay special attention to puppy proofing this area. Garages are notorious for housing hazardous chemicals that are deadly to pets. Antifreeze is a particular concern; look for a non-toxic brand. Tools, rags, car parts — anything that people normally keep in a garage — can become a danger if a puppy is around. Put these items well out of your puppy's reach.

In addition to puppy proofing your property, you will need to provide your young pup with plenty of supervision, for safety's sake as well as for socialization. Tap the times you're with your pup to work in some fun training and games that will shape his manners and give him an appropriate outlet for his high energy.

AN OUNCE OF PREVENTION

It takes time and effort, but puppy proofing your house in the first place is much easier than rushing your puppy to the vet for emergency surgery (not to mention the emotional and financial cost of such of trip). Veterinarians have removed a remarkable variety of objects from the stomachs and intestines of dogs of all ages, including pincushions (complete with pins), rubber balls, rocks, socks and underwear, ribbons, and plenty of splintered bones.

In many cases, a dog who dines without discretion and winds up on the operating table can make a full recovery, but any indigestible item can cause a potentially fatal intestinal blockage. Be alert to vomiting, distended abdomen, change in feces, drooling, or retching, and don't hesitate to take your dog to see your vet if you suspect he's eaten something he shouldn't have.

Looking Hangdog

Q My 10-year-old bichon frise sometimes goes to the bathroom in the house when no one is home. As soon as I walk in the front door, I know what Rascal has done without seeing the accident. She acts incredibly guilty, with downcast eyes and tail between her legs. If she feels so bad when she misbehaves, why does she continue to do it? Also, I think she sometimes urinates on the floor to get even with me for being gone for too long. The longer I'm away from home, the more likely she is to have an accident. Is she trying to get revenge?

A Many owners consider their pets to be members of the family, as well they should. But sometimes we take this idea too far by attaching human emotions and motives to our dog's behavior. Unlike humans, dogs don't feel guilty when they have done something we think is wrong. They do, however, react to our body language and tone of voice, and they quickly learn to read and respond to our emotions.

In Rascal's case, she has figured out that if she has an accident in the house, you will be angry when you get home. It's very simple in her mind because unlike a human, she can't grasp complicated ideas like, "I had an accident and five hours later, Mom is going to come home, see it, and get mad at me because now she has to clean it up." All Rascal knows is that if she has had an accident, you are angry when you come home. Dogs have no concept of cause and effect, so unfortunately, she doesn't realize that if she *didn't* go to the bathroom in the house, you would *not* be mad.

So if Rascal doesn't know she did something wrong, why does she look so guilty? Dogs often behave submissively when their owners are angry, in the hopes of ending the conflict. In wolf packs, subordinate members behave submissively in front of more dominant wolves to avoid fights. Rascal tucks her tail and hangs her head when she senses or anticipates your anger to illustrate her submissiveness to you, her pack leader. Signs of submissive behavior include a cringing posture, lowered ears, downcast eyes, and a tucked tail. A canine pack leader would most likely accept this behavioral apology and move on. Unhappily, people tend to become even angrier when confronted by such signs of "guilt," which makes the poor dog cringe even more.

As for the possibility of Rascal going to the bathroom in the house to get even with you for leaving her alone too long, dogs do not have the capacity to think in these terms. Revenge remains an exclusively human endeavor, and something only a complex brain can calculate. Dogs don't have the mental ability or the emotional complexity to grasp the concept of getting even.

Rascal's accidents are most likely the result of her inability to hold her urine for long periods of time. She may be suffering from a urinary tract infection or another medical condition that makes it hard for her to hold a full bladder for an extended period of time. Older dogs often have trouble with incontinence and sometimes need medication to remedy the problem. Take Rascal to your veterinarian for a complete physical evaluation. In the meantime, try not to leave her alone for too long to help her avoid accidents. This might mean asking a neighbor or professional pet sitter to come over and let her out in the yard to relieve herself on days you know you'll be gone for a long period of time.

> **BREED BYTE**
>
> The white, powder-puff bichon frise takes its name from a French term that means "curly lapdog."

Can You Dig It?

Q My five-year-old German shepherd-Lab mix has completely destroyed my garden with her digging. My yard looks like a minefield. I don't know what to do to stop her. As soon as my husband fills up the holes, Greta digs them up again. Why is she so obsessed with digging, and how can we make her stop?

A Many dogs love to dig in soft dirt or sand. I'm sure you've noticed how much Greta seems to be enjoying herself when she digs. In the wild, wolves and other canids dig to create dens for their pups or to hide food.

The instinct to dig remains strong in many domestic dogs who bury their bones or toys and scratch out cool places to rest during the summertime heat. Some dogs dig to burn off energy and relieve boredom. Unfortunately, digging, while not harmful to the dog, is destructive behavior that leaves owners frustrated and dogs in big trouble.

Before you can fix Greta's digging problem, you need to understand her motivation for digging. Does she spend a lot of time alone in your backyard? Do you take the time to play with her? Is she exercised regularly? Both German shepherds and Labrador retrievers are high-energy breeds who need fun and mentally stimulating activities to help wear them out. If you don't provide something for a dog like Greta to do, she will make her own fun, most likely in a way you don't appreciate. This is probably why she has taken up digging.

Digging can be a difficult habit to break, because dogs find it so enjoyable. The key to fixing this problem is to give Greta less destructive ways to burn off her energy while also discouraging her from tearing up the yard.

Start by protecting your garden. One method is to put large rocks on top of the areas where Greta likes to dig. Fill in the holes that Greta has dug, and place rocks on top of these spots. Dogs usually prefer soft dirt to carry out their excavations, so for larger areas, try spreading chicken wire out and staking it down while she learns to redirect her energy. Sprinkling or spraying the area with red pepper flakes, citronella or pennyroyal oil, or a commercial dog repellent will make the area less attractive. Trimming her nails may not curb the digging tendency, but could lessen the damage, so give her regular pedicures.

If Greta isn't already trained, enroll her in an obedience class. Most dogs need a job to do to occupy their minds, and both German shepherds and Labs have a strong work ethic as well as abundant energy. Teaching Greta obedience will give you control over her and give her something to think about besides digging, as well as building a closer relationship with you. If you have time, consider getting involved in a fun competitive canine activity like agility or fly ball. Greta would no doubt love to get involved in one of these high-energy sports. (See page 200 for more on canine sports.)

It is very important that you properly channel Greta's excess energy. If you need to leave her outside in the yard while you are away at work, take her for a long walk or play a vigorous game of fetch with her in the morning to tire her out. Provide her with alternatives to digging, such as a big rawhide bone or a hollow, hard rubber toy stuffed with treats, to occupy her time. Because she is a high-energy dog, she may need a diversion in the middle of the day to distract her from digging. Hire a professional pet sitter or dog walker, or ask a neighbor to come and play ball with Greta or take her on a long walk. Relieving her boredom and wearing her out physically will go a long way toward discouraging her digging instincts.

In addition to the above, you might compromise a bit and give Greta her own turf to tear up. Try taking a plastic kiddy pool (available at major discount chain stores for less than $10), filling it with dirt, and hiding a few dog biscuits for Greta to sniff out and discover through digging. If you catch her digging on your turf, clap your hands or do something to startle her so that she will stop digging and look at you. Then direct her to where she is allowed to dig. If you praise her for digging appropriately in her own patch of real estate filled with goodies, she will be more likely to ignore the rest of the yard.

Nipping the Herding Instinct

Q We have a two-year-old Shetland sheepdog named Casey. She is a wonderful dog except for one thing: She is always chasing our three young children. When the kids run and play in the backyard, Casey goes after them and nips at their heels. This really upsets the kids and they start to cry. Casey has torn their clothing and I'm afraid she is going to hurt one of them accidentally. Why does she do this and how can we stop her?

A Shetland sheepdogs belong to the class of herding breeds, which range in size from the shaggy Old English sheepdog to the stubby-legged corgi. My old corgi, Jazz, took great delight in rounding up my cats whenever one dared to slip through his doggy door into the backyard. He would herd the frustrated feline back to the door and sound the alert for me to check out his successful mission.

In your situation, Casey is simply fulfilling the legacy of her breed. Shelties were bred to herd livestock in their native Shetland Islands, off the coast of Scotland. They helped farmers move sheep from one pasture to another and along country roads to market. To get the sheep to comply, the dogs chased and nipped at their heels. Unfortunately, without sheep to attend to, Casey has chosen to herd your children. The rapid, erratic movements of children playing often trigger a herding dog's instincts.

This herding tendency is difficult, if not impossible, to suppress. Hundreds of years of breeding went into creating Casey's behavior, so it's not something she can just turn off. One solution is to use another form of play to divert her attention. When the kids start playing, engage Casey in a game of fetch. Many herding breed dogs will gladly give up trying to herd unruly children in favor of chasing a tennis ball or nosing a soccer ball or empty plastic jug around the yard. Of course, this only works if you are around to supervise. If you don't have time to play with her while the kids are running around the yard, your best approach is to remove the temptation and keep Casey in the house while the children are playing.

It's very likely, however, that Casey won't appreciate being shut out of the fun and will bark and whine at the door. Don't let her develop this habit. Practice some obedience work with her to get her attention off the children. If she refuses to be diverted, move her into a room where she can't see or hear the kids playing. If Casey is crate trained, this would be a good time to make use of the crate. Put her in the crate with a treat or toy and let her stay there until the kids have gone on to a more sedate activity. But do make sure that she has plenty of other opportunities to run and play — she is a young dog with lots of energy to burn. I recommend you spend five to ten minutes each day encouraging Casey to practice herding acceptable objects in an enclosed area such as a backyard.

However you choose to deal with this situation, it's imperative for you to do something to stop Casey's behavior. Although your dog may not intend to hurt your children, her nipping and chasing may well result in injury to one of your children or to one of their friends.

Have Nose, Must Travel

Q Whenever I take my beagle, Wesley, on a hike, he stops listening to me. We spent a long time in obedience class learning all the commands, and at home and in the park, he listens well. But when I take him on our weekend hikes to a local wilderness area and remove his leash, it's as if I don't exist. He puts his nose to the ground and takes off. I can yell, "Wesley, come!" until I lose my voice, but it does no good. I end up having to run after him and physically grab him to get his attention. I worry that he'll become so engrossed in sniffing that he will wander off and get hit by a car or get lost. Why does he act this way?

A Beagles, like all hound breeds, were bred specifically to track prey by following scent. The breed has been used for hundreds of years to hunt fox, rabbits, squirrels, and other small game. Hunters on horseback follow packs of these dogs, depending on them to locate the prey and corner it until the hunters can make the kill.

The olfactory power of Wesley's nose is about 10,000 times stronger than yours. That profound ability to detect the faintest scent and hundreds of years of breeding to track prey have created a dog that becomes completely focused on finding and hunting down game, no matter how many times you shout *Wesley, come!* This makes it tricky to control Wesley off-leash in a wilderness setting where the scents of rabbits, squirrels, and other animals prevail over your voice. You have a good foundation of obedience training at home, but now you need to work on training him to come when he's called in that distracting environment. Whatever you do, don't let him disregard your call. If you repeat *come* over and over again while he ignores you, you are only teaching him that he doesn't have to listen.

Because you must be able to reinforce the cue if Wesley isn't listening, begin working with him on a leash when you take him on hikes. Use a twenty-five-foot clothesline, rather than a standard six-foot leash. The longer line allows you to gradually give Wesley more distance between you as you work on teaching him to come when called from farther away, despite the distractions. Make sure that you select a wide-open area without trees or other objects that can tangle the leash.

Bring treats with you on your training sessions, and start by giving Wesley six feet of clothesline. Wait until he starts sniffing around, and then give him the *come* command. If he responds and comes to you, praise him heartily and give him a treat, and let him go off again. If he doesn't respond, "reel" him in on the line, but don't give him a treat. (Don't yell at him either!) When he is paying attention to you and coming reliably on six feet of line, give him a couple more feet of clothesline so he's farther away from you and repeat the exercise. If he ignores you, pull him toward you to make him come, but do not reward him when he gets to you. Go back to a shorter length of line and start over.

With practice, you should have Wesley responding when you call him from the end of the twenty-five-foot rope, each and every time. Once this is accomplished, you can try removing the leash to see if he will still come to you. Ultimately, you should gain more control over Wesley as he learns that he cannot continue whatever he is doing when you say *come*. Because beagles have such strong scenting and tracking instincts, however, Wesley may never be completely reliable off-leash in a wilderness area. If this turns out to be the case, keep him leashed when you are

LET'S SEE SOME ID

Think of microchipping as your dog's driver's license. No dog should be without one. Tags and even embroidered names and numbers on their collars are less effective than microchipping. All it takes is an open door for a dog to suddenly find himself lost. If your dog loses his collar, his chances of being reunited with you become slim. A microchip is permanent.

The procedure, done by your veterinarian, is quick and requires no anesthesia. A chip smaller than a grain of rice is inserted under the skin (usually between the shoulder blades) with a special needle. More and more veterinary clinics and animal shelters have special wands that they can wave over found dogs to detect these microchips, which have identification numbers that are registered with a national database. With the ID number, your dog's contact information is available to the clinic or shelter. Make sure you register with the microchip company and update your information if it changes.

hiking, for his own protection. (Make sure his collar has up-to-date tags. You might look into microchipping him, as well.) Otherwise, he may pick up a scent, take off after an animal, and find himself lost in the woods. Despite the stories of dogs finding their way home, most lost dogs, even ones with above-average scenting abilities, stay lost.

Desperately Seeking Celebrity Clone

Q I have wanted a Jack Russell terrier ever since I saw Eddie on the TV show *Frasier.* How can I find a Jack Russell that has the same personality as Eddie? Are most Jack Russells that smart, cute, and funny?

A The character of Eddie (played by a canine actor named Moose) certainly rates as one of the most endearing canine personalities of recent times. He plays tricks on his people, lets everyone know when he wants something, and rarely does anything wrong. He also spends a lot of time lounging around on the couch. Unfortunately, Eddie's delightful antics have given many viewers the impression that Jack Russell terriers are mellow, easy to train, and generally well behaved. This is rarely the case.

Television sitcoms such as *Frasier* and popular movies such as *101 Dalmatians* generally don't deal in reality, and that is particularly true when it comes to dog behavior. Let's discuss Jack Russells in particular, and then address the issue surrounding breeds popularized by Hollywood.

Although Eddie acts like a charmer on-screen, Moose the actor was abandoned twice by pet owners who couldn't deal with him before he was finally adopted by an expert in handling difficult dogs. I had the chance to meet Moose and his trainer a couple of times during fund-raising events for animal organizations. He loved the sound of cameras flashing and being surrounded by a crowd of two-legged admirers. He didn't, however, care to share the stage with other dogs, including Jack Russells. His trainer had to advise autograph-seekers not to bring their dogs up to meet Eddie when he "signed" his book, *My Life As a Dog.*

To understand the true nature of Jack Russell terriers (renamed Parson Russell terriers by the American Kennel Club), we need to look at their breed heritage. Developed in England hundreds of years ago to kill vermin, Jack Russells were bred to be fearless, energetic, tenacious hunters who were brave enough to attack badgers and other types of wildlife that often fought back. These dogs spent hours a day hunting and killing other animals, a job they learned to relish.

Fast forward to today's world and you have a big dog in a small package who is always looking for trouble. Many

Jack Russells have a very strong hunting instinct, which makes it difficult for them to live with cats and other small dogs. They also have a very independent nature, as they were bred to work alone all day and make their own decisions as they hunted. The result is that they don't take direction well, meaning they can be notoriously difficult to train. Many Jack Russells also have a strong alpha temperament, which makes them want to be the boss in just about every situation.

If you have your heart set on getting a particular dog based on a movie or TV show, learn more about the breed and meet some of these dogs before you go out and get one. Realize what you are getting into; chances are good that you won't get a dog that is anything like the one on the screen. Especially if this will be your first dog, you should seriously consider choosing a breed that fits your lifestyle and experience, not just one who looks and acts cute on TV.

Jack Russells and other movie star breeds like Dalmatians can be difficult to handle even for experienced dog owners. First-time owners often find these dogs overwhelming, which is one reason so many of them end up in animal shelters. Other breeds can tax your patience, too, but may have a greater likelihood of adapting to family life. The lovable and very popular Labrador retriever, for example, sports oodles of energy and needs an owner willing to spend the time to train and to provide suitable activities. Take the time to make sure a particular breed is right for you.

Silver and the Strangers

BECKY AND HAL CONTACTED ME after an incident in which their nine-month-old Australian shepherd, without perceived warning, suddenly lunged and nipped a friend in their home. Silver was a reserved puppy, but as he matured, he developed a blend of dominance and fear aggression toward strangers. Behavior problems often appear or intensify in adolescence as young dogs test their independence and their position in the family hierarchy. It is also a time when fear issues can surface.

I determined that Silver was aggressive partly because of insufficient leadership from his owners. Australian shepherds can be shy and reactive as "teenagers," especially if they don't have owners who set limits and teach self-control. Allowing himself to be petted, then "thinking" about it and biting without provocation suggests he was fearful, but confident enough to act on his insecurities. Silver's attack on their friend, whom he did not know, indicated that he was protecting Becky.

While we worked to counter Silver's behavior toward strangers, it was vital to keep him from biting again. Apart from the obvious danger, Silver viewed an attack as a victory, which reinforced his unacceptable actions. For walks, we fitted Silver with a halter collar so he would heed his owners. We also incorporated the use of a basket muzzle to help Becky and Hal relax when Silver was near other people. We made wearing the basket muzzle more appealing by placing special treats in it and inviting Silver to take them. He didn't see the basket as punishment, and the couple felt safer having him out in public and around others. As they worked with Silver, their change in body language also helped turn the dog's attitude around.

In order to elevate Becky and Hal's leadership status in Silver's eyes, we began the "Nothing in Life is Free" program (see Paying the Price, page 156). Instead of calling the shots, Silver had to *earn* his meals, playtime, and affection by heeding basic obedience commands. This program taught Silver to view the couple as his leaders and guides, rather than resources that he felt compelled to protect.

The couple increased Silver's exercise to provide him with a suitable outlet for his energy and enrolled him in obedience training, agility, and herding classes, which engaged his intelligence, increased his confidence level, and sharpened his ability to respond quickly and appropriately to his owners. We also incorporated desensitization and counterconditioning techniques to help Silver learn that strangers weren't a threat. Given Silver's work ethic, Becky put him in "work mode" so that he focused on her rather than worrying about driving the strangers away. Today, Becky and Hal describe Silver as a different dog.

Contributed by Alice Moon-Fanelli, PhD

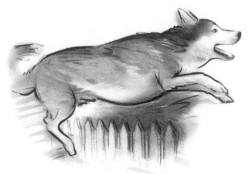

Poof! Disappearing Dog Act

Q Our Siberian husky, Tundra, is six years old and is always escaping from our yard. He used to dig out from under the fence, so we removed some of the dirt at the base of the fence line and put cement there. This stopped him from digging out, but then he found a way to open the gate. We put a lock on the gate, and now he jumps over the fence. No matter what we do to stop him, he finds a way to escape. We have finally started locking him in the garage when we aren't home because we tired of going to the animal shelter to pick him up all the time. Why does he run away? Should we take this as a sign that he doesn't like living here?

A Tundra sounds like a tenacious escape artist who is determined to spend his time checking out the neighborhood. It's doubtful that this is because he doesn't like living with you. It's more likely that when he's alone, he feels compelled to provide his own amusement. The fact that Tundra is a Siberian husky also contributes to his tendency to roam. Huskies were bred to travel vast distances pulling sleds and to think for themselves while they worked. When Tundra decides to leave your yard, he is responding to his inbred urge to travel and be independent.

When I first adopted Chipper, her husky heritage frequently helped her magically disappear from my yard, but the golden retriever in her seemed to coax her back home to my front porch. She has managed to open locks from inside grooming cages and once even pawed open a dead bolt and doorknob to exit a hotel room in Colorado.

You can take several steps to curb Tundra's roaming, in addition to the excellent measures you have already employed. First, make sure Tundra is neutered. Male dogs are notorious for doing everything possible to escape their homes in order to search for females in heat. If Tundra is still intact, this could be the biggest source of your problem. Have him neutered right away and keep him confined until his raging hormones subside.

It sounds as if Tundra performs his escape routines when you aren't home and he's alone in the backyard. He is probably bored or lonely or both. Before you leave him for long periods of time, give him some vigorous exercise to tire him out. A rousing game of fetch or a long jog (if you are so inclined) can do wonders to burn off some of his excess energy and make him less likely to run away.

Physical exercise and mentally stimulating games will also reduce Tundra's frustration level. Make sure you leave him several chew toys or food puzzle toys to amuse himself with and change them frequently to keep him interested.

Loneliness can motivate a dog to escape his yard in the hopes of finding companionship. Huskies, more than many breeds, are pack animals, bred to work in a group and to be around other dogs. Try hiring a professional pet sitter or a responsible, dog-friendly neighborhood teen to come over in the afternoon to take Tundra for a walk or play fetch with him in the yard. Breaking up the isolation of his day will help reduce his desire to leave your yard in search of companionship. If you have the room and the financial ability, a second dog, if compatible with Tundra, might be the perfect solution.

Tundra's wandering attitude will probably benefit from some training as well. Enroll him in an obedience class so both of you can learn the basics. Obedience training will reinforce the bond between you and help him see you as his pack leader. If Tundra feels more connected to you emotionally, he'll be less likely to want to leave your home.

In addition, you might want to secure your yard even further to stave off any more of Tundra's escape attempts. Since he has taken to jumping over the fence, consider adding chicken wire at the top that is slanted inward at a 90-degree angle to the fence. Tundra will find it very difficult, if not impossible, to jump over the fence with this extension blocking his exit.

Stop, Shoe Thief!

Q My three-year-old dachshund, Schotzi, goes into my closet when I'm not home and takes my shoes out to chew on them. I try to keep the closet door closed, but if I inadvertently leave it open even just a few inches, she pushes it open with her nose and drags out a shoe and destroys it. Why is she so obsessed with shoes, and how can I stop this bad (and expensive) habit?

A I'm guessing the shoes in your closet that Schotzi prefers are made of leather. Many dogs find the smell and texture of leather intoxicating. They love the way it feels and tastes when they chew on it. Some people make the mistake of giving old shoes to puppies to chew on when they are little, expecting the pup to know the difference between an old shoe that's okay to chew and a newer shoe that is off-limits. If Schotzi was given old shoes to gnaw on when she was little, she learned at an early age that shoes are made for chewing. Now, when she wants to gnaw on something, she simply helps herself from your wardrobe.

Even if you didn't give Schotzi shoes when she was a puppy, she is choosing something that smells like you and that reassures her in your absence. Many dogs deal with loneliness or separation anxiety by seeking out their owner's belongings (to dogs, even a stinky shoe is a comforting reminder of their owners).

Your first task is to make sure you don't tempt her by leaving your closet door ajar. You might try putting self-closing hinges on the closet door or even closing your bedroom door as well. You could store your shoes on shelves above her reach or in a hanging container with pockets that hangs on the back of the door. Next, give her something else to chew. Since she has a penchant for leather, consider a rawhide chew toy as a replacement. (Talk to your veterinarian first to make sure rawhide is safe for your dog.) Just before you leave the house, give Schotzi one of these rawhide chews and praise her heartily when she starts working on it. If she isn't interested at first, a dab of peanut butter or a smear of cheese on the chew will probably increase its attractiveness.

In the event that Schotzi does sink her teeth into one of your shoes, and you catch her in the act, take it away from her (have you taught her the *leave it!* command? See Ignoring Temptation, page 169.) and trade it for the rawhide chew. In time, she will get the message that shoes are a *no* and rawhides are a *yes*.

If Schotzi is one of those rare dogs who does not like to chew on rawhide, you may need to try a different chew toy to get her attention off your shoes. Take a trip to your local pet supply store and bring her with you. Walk her through the aisles and see which chew toys interest her the most. By letting her pick out her own chew toy, you are making her an active participant in her retraining.

Undercover Agent

Q My dachshund, Bogart, makes us laugh with his bedtime ritual. Whatever the weather, he insists on burying his entire body under the covers and sleeping at our feet. To make it a challenge, we've tried tucking the sheets and bedspread in tightly, but he still manages to wiggle his way in. I worry that he won't get enough oxygen being so deep under the covers. Why does he do this and can it be harmful?

A Bogart belongs to a great breed that was born to dig. Although affectionately known as "wiener dogs" because of their long backs and short legs, dachshund actually means "badger dog" in German. These funny, curious, and determined dogs were bred to dig for burrowing mammals and to take on badgers and other large varmints, climbing out of the hole triumphantly clutching their prey in their mouths. Designed so that their teeth — not their toes — are the first body parts that come in contact with prey deep in a hole, dachshunds are fierce fighters.

As for the bedtime ritual, wiggling into tight places (like under the covers) comes naturally to Bogart and feels cozy. As long as he doesn't disturb your sleep or nip your toes, let him continue this nighttime ritual. Don't worry — he can breathe under the sheets and will emerge if he becomes uncomfortable.

Tossing and Twitching All Night

Q My family gets the biggest kick out of watching our six-year-old Lab, Barnaby, sleep. Not only does he snore — loudly — but also his outstretched paws move and he twitches all over. Sometimes he yelps or whimpers, but his eyes stay closed. Watching and listening to him when he is sleeping makes us wonder if dogs dream and, if so, what do they dream about?

A Compared with us, dogs are regular Rip Van Winkles. They sleep at least twelve hours a day and rarely suffer from insomnia. At night, they seem to nod off before you even have time to set your snooze alarm. Not all dogs snore like Barnaby, but it is fairly common for dogs to twitch their paws and make noises when they are asleep. Some dogs move their legs as if they were in full stride, perhaps chasing a rabbit. Look closely at Barnaby and you might also notice the twitching of his eyelids and whiskers, indicating that he has fallen into the deep sleep stage. But dogs don't stay in that deep slumber for long. Most of the time, they sleep lightly and are aware of their surroundings.

Sleep experts report that dogs do indeed dream. The big mystery is their topics of choice when they drift off into dreamland. We can only guess that they dream about activities like trips to the dog park, chowing down on their favorite treat, or finally catching a speedy, elusive squirrel.

Some scientists speculate that dogs may dream primarily of smells. That holds merit. After all, we dream visually because sight is our dominant sense. Dogs rely on their noses more than their eyes. They smell objects before they look, hear, touch, or taste them. It may be a long time before we figure out a way to identify our dogs' dreams, but it is a strong bet that since much of a dog's brain is associated with scents, it is a dream filled with lots of canine-welcoming smells.

Stashing Away for a Rainy Day

Q My Brittany spaniel, Chelsea, has a weird habit. When I feed her kibble, she picks up each piece from her bowl and places it on the kitchen floor or in other rooms of the house. After she has removed all the kibble from her bowl, she tracks down each piece throughout the house and eats it. Why does she do this?

A Chelsea's odd eating habits are a throwback to her ancient roots as a hunter and scavenger. Her ancestors could not count on people to serve them two meals each day. Because food was not always available to wolves and other wild dogs whenever they needed it, they would stash parts of their kill in various places so they could return to it later when they were hungry and couldn't find prey. Some domestic dogs, particularly hunting breeds like spaniels, still retain this instinct. In fact, some dogs will actually hide each piece of kibble in corners or under furniture before they go back and eat it.

Even though Chelsea receives regular meals, this ancient instinct is telling her to stash the kibble in different places so she can return to it later to eat it. Of course, "later" may only be a few minutes after she has performed her food-relocation ritual. But in Chelsea's mind, her behavior helps ensure a constant source of food in the future. Chipper does this occasionally with her chew bones. She will sit politely for me to hand over the meaty treat and then dash out the doggy door to bury it in the backyard.

To human observers, this food-spreading behavior doesn't make sense unless you think about the instinct that is driving it. Just remember as you watch Chelsea spread her food around that she is heeding the call of the wild. If you don't want kibble surprises all over your house, I recommend that you keep bedroom and bathroom doors closed during feeding time. Stepping on hard kibble with bare feet is no delight!

PART II

What Are You Talking About?

It's easy to fall into the notion

that people are superior to the rest of the animal kingdom because of our ability to talk. Some of us speak more than one language. Some of us know many megasyllable words and can even pronounce them. Some of us, in fact, never seem to *stop* talking! That's all great when it comes to speaking people-to-people.

As much as we may view ourselves as accomplished linguists, the truth is that our dogs are the truly stellar communicators, and often without uttering a single bark or yip. In dog-to-dog discussions, there is rarely a communication miscue. Dogs are more consistent in their "talk" than we are. They don't tell lies and they don't hide their feelings.

Dogs do their best to convey their canine cues to us, but sometimes we fail to interpret their signals accurately. There is no "dogtionary" published yet, but we can improve our communication with our canine pals if we learn some of their "language." Along the way, we may commit a canine faux pas or two, but that's all right. After all, we're only human.

Canine Conversation

Q My dog is a very vocal miniature schnauzer. At times, it seems like we are actually carrying on a conversation. I never knew that dogs could make so many different sounds. She has several different barks, she whines, and she even makes singing sounds. How can I better understand what she is saying?

A Miniature schnauzers are among the chattiest of breeds. Like many of their terrier cousins, they were originally bred to bark, or speak up, as a way of alerting their owners to rats or other rodents in the home and while going to ground after small game when hunting. Beagles and other hound breeds bark to answer back to their two-legged hunting companions. Corgis, Australian shepherds, and other herding breeds yap to control the comings and goings of sheep, cattle, and other livestock.

Although dogs communicate primarily with nonverbal body language, they are capable of a wide range of sounds. There is always a purpose for their barks, even if the reason is sheer boredom. These sounds have consistent meanings, based on the pitch, pace, and overall tones. Here is a list of some common dog sounds.

◆ **HIGH-PITCHED, LONG BARK.** "I'm worried or lonely and need assurance."

◆ **RAPID, HIGH-PITCHED, REPETITIVE BARKS.** "Let's play! Chase me! At least throw my ball!"

◆ **LOW, REPETITIVE BARKS.** "Stay away from my family! Keep off my property!"

◆ **A SINGLE BARK OR TWO.** "Hey! I'm here! What are you doing?"

◆ **GROWLING WITH TEETH EXPOSED AND TENSE BODY LEANING FORWARD.** "I'm warning you — back off and leave me alone."

◆ **GROWLING WITH BODY CROUCHED LOW.** "You're making me nervous. If you come too close, I might snap at you."

◆ **SINGSONG HOWLING.** "Hey, calling all canines! Who's out there? What's going on?"

◆ **SQUEAKY, REPETITIVE YAPS OR WHINES.** "I'm hurt or scared or feeling stressed. I need attention!"

Okay to Growl in Play?

Q When I play fetch with my two-year-old golden retriever, she sometimes lets out a little growl when I reach for the ball. She looks at me sideways, seems to have an open-mouth grin, puts her butt high in the air, and stretches her front paws out. Even though she is growling, is she being playful? Or challenging?

A From the body postures you describe, your dog is thoroughly happy to be playing with you. She is showing you the "play bow" position (front legs splayed out, head lowered, rear end elevated). Her alert expression and throaty noise are friendly invites for you to continue trying to grab the ball from her and tossing it. She regards you as a valued playmate.

Playtime with your dog provides a golden opportunity to improve your communication and practice good manners. When your dog is in a playful mood, use the chance to reinforce some basic behaviors, such as *sit, wait,* and *leave it.* Have her heed these cues before getting a reward, in this case, the tennis ball. Finally, you decide when the game is over, not your dog. This reinforces your position as leader.

THE NAME GAME

Stumped by what to call your new dog? You can go with the majority by dubbing her Molly or him Max — two of the most popular canine monikers. If you want to be more original, here are some recommendations.

◆ Stick with a two-syllable name ending in a vowel, like Buddy or Gracie.

◆ Select a name you enjoy saying out loud — not an embarrassing one like Poopsie.

◆ Consider names associated with something you enjoy, like Chipper or Lily.

◆ Avoid names that sound too much like *no* such as Joe or Flo.

◆ Link the name to your dog's personality: Happy, Frisky, or Speedy.

Make sure your dog associates his name with positive experiences. Use it when you play, feed, and cuddle with your new dog. Resist saying his name when you need to stop a behavior like digging or barking.

Strictly Dog to Dog

Q Whenever my husky mix, Jessie, meets a new dog, she goes through a whole ritual of posturing. Usually, the hair on her spine goes up. She marches up to the newcomer at our dog park in silence. She sniffs the dog's rear end and often places her head over the other dog's back. Sometimes she will make some quick growling noises, but within a few minutes, the two are playing chase and then sharing a water bowl. I know my dog is not aggressive, but I find myself always having to explain to other dog owners that this is just how Jessie meets other dogs. Is this normal dog behavior?

A Jessie behaves a lot like Chipper does. Dominant dogs, especially female ones, like to know right away who the boss is. Sometimes, after their initial introduction, the other dog dominates Chipper, who accepts being first mate rather than the captain of the canine dog park. Other times, Chipper is in charge.

Dogs have only elementary verbal language but very sophisticated body language. Their body language involves every part of their body from nose to tip of tail, and every dog knows how to read it. Just as we put words together to form a meaningful message, dogs read two or three body cues together to make an understandable dog message.

When dogs first meet, they often quickly size each other up without a single bark. They sniff each other, eye each other, and within seconds know each other's sex, age, health condition, and position in the canine hierarchy. Just as you described, the dominant dog will loom her head over the back of the submissive one. There is a moment of stillness as the two dogs study one another. Both understand this posturing and will generally accept their social rankings. Sometimes some snarling will occur or a brief scuffle, usually over in seconds, will break out — but sometimes a serious fight can ensue.

This form of behavior is far different from what you see when two canine chums greet one another. During friendly reunions, familiar dogs will sniff each other's faces and rear ends but may also jump up and touch front paws in midair or playfully mouth their pal's neck or tug on their cheek. Notice their mouths. Happy, relaxed dogs keep their mouths open. Tense, alert dogs keep their mouths tightly closed.

Even though you describe Jessie as not aggressive, pay close attention to new doggy introductions at the dog park and other places. Many dogs are more territorial when leashed, but it's always best to have them under control when they first meet. Explain that Jessie can be a little snappy at first but that she usually makes friends. If the dog park protocol is for dogs to run loose, stay nearby while Jessie introduces herself. While dogs will usually sort things out for themselves pretty quickly, you need to be close enough to break up a fight if the other dog turns out to be as assertive as Jessie is.

Are Dogs "Word Worthy"?

Q When I talk to my dog, Charlie, he usually cocks his head, as if he is really listening and understanding what I'm telling him. Do dogs know words, or is he just listening to the tone of my voice?

A Dogs read your voice tone more than the actual words to gauge if you're delivering praise or discipline. Try this test with Charlie. Stiffen your muscles, grab a telephone book, and begin to call out the names alphabetically in a stern, low tone in front of him. Watch his response. I bet he will glance your way, crouch down, and move away from you, almost as if to say, "I can tell you're angry but I'm not sure why."

Now repeat the exercise, but this time, relax your muscles, sit on the floor, and call out the names in the phone book in a cheery, musical tone. Watch what Charlie does. He will probably race over to you with a circular wag and a happy, open-mouth grin and try to give you kisses.

The same words spoken in a different tone elicit different reactions from your dog. Although tone matters more, many dogs do understand specific words and phrases. That's because we have been consistent when speaking these words followed by a particular action. Chipper licks her muzzle whenever I say to her, "Want to eat?" because she knows a goodie is coming. At night, when I say, "Find your spot!" Chipper races upstairs and flops on her bed in my bedroom. Her motivation? She receives a tasty nighttime snack each time she complies.

You can train your four-legged vocabulary builder to perform some nifty tricks by using treats and praise to reinforce desired responses. For example, let's say you want to wow your pals when they visit by telling your dog to give you the sports section from your newspaper. This is easier to accomplish than you may realize. Start by placing several sections of your daily newspaper on the floor in order, such as the front page, the local news, sports, and features.

Alert your dog to pay attention. Put a small treat on the sports section. Point to the sports section while saying, "Find the sports page." When your dog's nose touches the sports section to pick up the treat, say "sports page" and praise him. Do this several times in a row for a few days, and then gradually remove the treat, but continue saying, "Find the sports page." Offer the treat after your dog touches the sports pages. In time, your dog will learn the order of the newspaper sections and always go to the third one — the one with all the scores. He will score a hit with your friends.

RICO THE WONDER DOG

In a 2005 study published in *Science,* German researchers reported that Rico, a Border collie, comprehends more than 200 words — a vocabulary size similar to that of trained apes, dolphins, and parrots. Rico can fetch at least 200 objects by name and seems able to expand his word knowledge bank.

Rico's ability to learn new words is explained by a process known as fast mapping. This technique allows dogs to form a quick and rough hypothesis about the meaning of a new word after a single exposure to the item in question. The experimenters sent Rico into a room that contained eight items, seven of which were familiar to him. Rico did not know the name of the eighth object, but in seven out of ten tests, he appropriately retrieved a different novel item. That's one smart dog!

Spelling Champ

Q Our dog gets so excited whenever we say the words "treat" or "walk" that we've started to spell them out. But now it seems like she understands when we spell out "t-r-e-a-t" or "w-a-l-k." She starts to jump around, wiggle, and squeal with delight. We are amazed that she responds. Is our dog a speller?

A Many dog owners try to outwit their dogs by coming up with a secret code for objects and events that are highly prized by dogs, such as treat, walk, and car ride. It is natural to switch to spelling to tone down the emotional outbursts of pure delight from a dog on constant alert for her favorite words. But think about how these words became such favorites in the first place. Dogs quickly learn to associate the word "treat" with the tasty biscuit or dog cookie that you hand over. They soon catch on that "walk" leads to you reaching for the leash and heading to the front door.

By spelling out these key words every time you provide a treat or take her for a trek to the park, your dog links these sounds with their meanings. She can't spell, but she is good at spotting predictable, consistent behaviors by you. Knowing this, you can expand your dog's vocabulary and wow your friends by associating specific spelled-out words with specific actions. Your dog could "understand" that "t-a-l-k" means you want him to let out a woof and that "r-e-m-o-t-e" means that you want him to fetch the television remote for you.

I imagine if you looked blankly at your dog and spelled out "e-n-c-y-c-l-o-p-e-d-i-a" in a calm tone without moving, your dog might listen politely but wouldn't rush for the treat jar or grab the leash. And certainly, she will never hound your bookshelf in search of an encyclopedia or beat you in a game of Scrabble!

New Dog: Friend or Foe?

Q Whenever I meet a new dog, even one belonging to friends, I get a bit nervous. As a child, I was bitten by a neighbor's dog. It was bad enough that I needed stitches. I love animals but always find myself hesitating before greeting a dog for the first time, even a small one. I guess it is hard to shake childhood memories, but I don't want to be unduly afraid or nervous around dogs. What signs can I look for to determine if the dog is friendly or not? How should I approach a dog I'm meeting for the first time?

A I sympathize, since I was also bitten by a dog when I was a child. In fact, children far outnumber burglars and mail carriers as victims of dog bites. It is okay to acknowledge your fear and to be a bit cautious when meeting a dog for the first time. That's being safe and smart.

When greeting dogs, especially ones you don't know, avoid a head-on stare. Sustained eye contact can be threatening to any dog. Also, do not hover over the dog, pat him on the head, or try to give him a bear hug — these are potentially threatening gestures to dogs. Extend the back of your hand slowly to allow the dog the opportunity to sniff and approach you.

To "read" a dog, you must size up the entire body language of the dog and not rely on just one physical cue. Here are some head-to-tail signs to note when meeting a new dog.

◆ **EARS.** Challenging or dominant dogs keep their ears erect, tense, and pointed forward. Calm, contented dogs tend to relax their ears. Fearful or worried dogs often pull their ears flat against their heads.

◆ **EYES.** Direct staring by a dog means confidence and, possibly, dominance. Dogs who look at you and then look away are indicating that they are yielding power to you. Dogs who greet you with "soft eyes" are content. Large, dilated pupils can be a sign of fear or aggression, especially in conditions when the lighting should make the pupils contract.

- **MOUTH.** A soft, relaxed mouth indicates a relaxed dog. A tight mouth or tensed-up lips show tension. A curled lip and exposed teeth may be signs of aggression or, in the case of certain breeds like Chesapeake Bay retrievers, could be signs of smiling. Tongue flicking often means a feeling of uncertainty or uneasiness. Yawning usually indicates stress, not fatigue. Yawning helps lower a dog's blood pressure to help him stay calm. Dogs who mouth your hand without using their teeth are delivering a friendly greeting. However, adult dogs who use their teeth are challenging your authority.

- **TORSO TENSION.** Muscle tension is your barometer to the emotions being conveyed by a dog. Tightened muscles, especially around the head and shoulders, often indicate a dog who is scared or aggressive.

- **GESTURES.** Play bowing (chest down, front legs extended, back end up, tail wagging) is the universal canine sign for happiness and an invitation to play. Nudging you with a nose is a plea for affection or a cue that you're in his chair and could you please move. Lifting a paw often means "let's play" or "pay attention to me."

◆ **FUR.** A calm dog displays a smooth coat from his shoulders to his hips. A scared or challenged dog often elevates the hairs (called hackles) along his spine to appear larger in size.

◆ **TAIL.** An alert dog holds his tail tall and erect. A fearful dog tucks his tail between his legs. An excited dog hoists his tail high and wags it quickly from side to side. A cautious or nervous dog holds his tail straight out and wags it slowly and steadily. A contented dog keeps his tail relaxed and at ease.

When in doubt, accept the most fearful or aggressive signal. If the back end is acting friendly and the tail is wagging, but the dog is grimacing and looks tense, assume the most dangerous end is telling the truth. If there is fear in any body language sign, then fear is the answer. Better to be safe and greet that dog from a distance.

Terrier Tum-Tum

Q My husband and I did a lot of research on various breeds before choosing a dog. We decided on a rare breed called Glen of Imaal terrier because of the breed's sturdiness, compact size, and non-shedding coat. We adopted a spirited puppy we named Byline, who is now eight months old. As a first-time dog owner, I don't "speak" dog very well. Sometimes, when Byline flops down and goes belly up, he seems to love me giving him belly scratches. Other times, however, he responds to my belly scratches by growling slightly. How can I better understand what Byline is trying to convey to me?

A Congratulations on the new addition to your family. I applaud you for taking the time to research the breeds before making a decision about the one that best suits your lifestyle. As for learning "dog speak," you cannot focus on just one part of a dog's body and expect to accurately interpret what Byline is trying to tell you. You have to look at the whole package and size up the situation. You also need to take into account the personality traits of terrier breeds. Although there are always exceptions, terriers tend to be bossy and need to know that you are in charge. Terriers heed owners who are clear and consistent in their body and word cues.

Let me illustrate with the belly flop, a common canine posture. When a dog rolls on his back and exposes his belly, most owners perceive this as a sign of submission. But pay close attention to the dog's posture and muscle tension. A dog who goes into a shoulder roll and stays tucked, with belly up, muscles relaxed, tongue flicking, and eyes looking at you sideways, is usually submissive. These are good, consistent cues to let you know Byline wants his belly rubbed.

But a dog who openly flops on his back with belly exposed and muscles tight, while staring directly at you and perhaps talking or growling slightly, is a confident dog calling the shots and demanding that you pay attention and do what he wants. At eight months, Byline is at an age when he is trying to determine his ranking in his "pack" — that is, in your household. You need to be in charge. If Byline starts to stare and tighten his muscles while you are rubbing his belly, stand up and have him *sit* for you. When he does, praise him briefly and then walk away. These actions tell Byline that you are the leader.

I strongly encourage you to enroll Byline in a basic obedience class taught by a professional trainer who uses positive reinforcement techniques. Byline is at a challenging adolescent age and would benefit greatly from this type of class. He will learn good doggy manners that will last him a lifetime.

Loves to Lick

Q I adore my golden retriever, but she showers me with affection. She is constantly licking my face, my hands, even my toes! Why use the bathtub when she's around? How can I tone down her greetings and still let her know I appreciate her?

A You have what I call a "Licky Lou" type of dog. When I first adopted Chipper, she was a sloppy, persistent kisser as well! I'm happy to see that you are concerned about not snuffing out her enthusiastic joy for you. That is very important. Don't worry, it is possible to teach her other ways to show her affection.

First, recognize that your dog is doing what comes naturally. Puppies instinctively lick their mothers' chins and faces in their constant quest for chow. (Hey, these are fast-growing critters!) Many experts suggest this behavior dates back to the days when female wolves would hunt and devour their prey before returning to their litters, because it was easier to travel on a full stomach than lug a heavy rabbit home. Their hungry pups would lick their faces to cause them to regurgitate this barely digested food.

But face licking goes beyond the need to eat. Puppies are also conveying that they recognize and honor the elevated stature of adult dogs. Pay attention the next time you go to a dog park or other place with friendly dogs. Notice the ones who come up to others, lower their posture a bit, and gently kiss the muzzle of the other dog. It is their way of saying, "Hey, you rule. Now, wanna play chase?"

When it comes to licking people, sometimes the motivation may be a bit of leftover gravy that draws the attention of our dogs. However, the main reason some dogs shower their owners with kisses is what Aretha Franklin sings about: R-E-S-P-E-C-T. Even as they age, many dogs regard their people as leaders of their pack, the two-legger who deserves admiration. Take it as a canine compliment. Your dog is seeking your attention and your approval.

The amount of canine kissing depends on a dog's personality. Strong-willed and adventure-seeking dogs tend to dole out kisses less frequently than sociable, happy-to-meet-all dogs who lick to acknowledge that you outrank them. Some breeds, like golden retrievers, are very mouth-oriented and express themselves by unleashing a kissing barrage.

So, how do you stop succumbing to impromptu doggy baths? Forget about pushing your dog away after that first "kiss." Odds are this action will only motivate her to deliver more licks because she thinks she failed to communicate her message the first time. Or, she may perceive it as a signal to play and heap on more sloppy kisses.

Your best options are to teach your dog the *kiss* and *stop* commands. Your goal is to acknowledge your dog's strong desire to display her feelings toward you while maintaining your rank as top dog. You also need some backup aids, such as chew toys, to offer as appropriate distractions for "oral-minded" dogs.

Conduct mini-training sessions during quiet times, such as when your dog just wakes up, after a long walk, or any time when she and you are in a calm mood (not when you've just walked in the door!). Allow her to lick your face or hand once, say *good kiss,* and give her a small treat. Repeat a few times. Now, you're ready to teach her the *stop* command. When she moves toward licking you, put your hand in front of her face like a traffic cop halting cars and say *stop.* If she doesn't lick, dole out a treat and praise her.

It can be tough to try to bottle the enthusiasm of a tail-wagger who is happy to see you after you've been gone for way-too-many-hours, so you also need to teach your dog a more acceptable greeting than a face bath. Teach her to shake paws or perform a trick, such as sitting up or fetching a favorite toy when you come in the door. In time, she will learn that the big payoffs — your affection and a tasty treat — occur when she has licked her licking habit.

Look Out for Launching Lab!

Q Our very happy two-year-old Labrador retriever, Nacho, can be a little too excited when she greets people entering our front door. When the doorbell rings, she races to the door. Try as we may, we are unable to stop her as she leaps up and puts her front paws on the shoulders of our house guests. Nacho weighs 75 pounds and has knocked down a few guests with her leaps. What can we do to keep her from jumping up on people? We don't want her to cause an injury.

A A leaping Lab can generate as much force as a determined linebacker tackling a quarterback. Although your dog's intentions are friendly, unlike the linebacker's, the results can be the same, with the recipient of the "hit" landing on the ground, hard.

First, you need to understand why Nacho leaps. In the dog world, leaping up and greeting another dog face to face is an accepted form of friendly communication. Watch two dogs who are pals play together. They may behave like a couple of stallions with their front paws touching up high as they romp. Many dogs transfer this canine hello to people in a bid for attention.

When our dogs are pups, we often mistakenly encourage them to leap up to greet us. It's hard to resist a cute, 10-pound Lab pup when she stretches her front paws up to your thigh to say "hi." By reaching down and responding with a hug or a pat on the head, we inadvertently instill in our fast-growing canines that this is an acceptable behavior.

Nacho is not too old to relearn proper doggy greetings toward houseguests and people she meets with you during walks and other outings. Curb the leaping by teaching her *off* and *sit*. Start by putting Nacho on a head-type collar (such as a Gentle Leader or Halti) and a leash six feet or longer in length. Ask a friend to enter your home, without acknowledging the dog in any way. As Nacho races to deliver an airborne "hello," gently but firmly turn the leash so that Nacho must turn her head toward you. Firmly say *off!* This grounds her and keeps her from touching your friend.

When she stops trying to jump and sits down, immediately say *good sit!* and give her a treat or praise. Repeat this sequence a few times in a row to help Nacho understand what earns her praise and a tasty reward. Expand this tutorial by enlisting other friends to come in and wait to greet Nacho until she sits politely.

Once Nacho has mastered the sit on a leash, you can teach her to sit politely at a rug near your door to greet guests. Like most Labs, Nacho sounds like a very social dog. You may not want to snuff out her desire to greet guests, but if you use *off* and *sit* consistently, she will be able to welcome visitors without bowling them over.

Neighborhood Noisemaker

Q My new next-door neighbors leave their very noisy Sheltie in their backyard during the day while they are at work. He yaps and yips constantly, and his bark is so sharp and piercing that it hurts my ears. I operate a home business and have to shut my windows and turn on the radio to muffle the nonstop noise. What can I do to restore peace in my neighborhood?

A Opt for a little diplomacy and neighborhood friendliness first. Introduce yourself to your new neighbors and engage them in conversation. Ask them about their dog and his personality. Tactfully ask why he stays out in the backyard and tell them that he barks a lot during the day. Although Shelties are known as vocal breeds, you'd be surprised at how many people are unaware that their dogs are big barkers when they are away from home. Some assume that their dog barks only when they're at home to alert them of someone approaching their property.

Without being nasty, inform them that you work from home and that you sincerely want to work together for a solution. The key is not to put them in a defensive posture, from which they won't listen to what you are saying. Try mentioning the fact that some dogs bark out of boredom and the need for exercise. Depending on where you live, backyard dogs can be at risk for being teased, stolen, or even attacked by coyotes. They can dig under fences and escape and possibly be hit by a vehicle.

Provide your neighbors with some remedies. Ask if it might be possible for the dog to stay inside and have access to a doggy door for bathroom breaks. Suggest they give their Sheltie long-lasting treats like a hollow, hard rubber toy stuffed with cheese, kibble, or peanut butter. Ask them if they have considered taking their dog to a day care for a day or more each week. A tired dog is a happy, quiet one.

In addition, your new neighbors may not realize there are special collars designed to control excessive barking.

These collars come in many forms. Please do not suggest an anti-bark collar that relies on electric shock or vibrations; they are cruel. Instead, suggest pain-free types that contain citronella oil. When a dog barks while wearing this type of collar, the noise triggers the release of citrus scent. Dogs detest this smell and usually stop barking. These collars are ideal for use on dogs when owners are not within sight or sound. But experts caution against using these collars on dogs who are anxious, because the citrus sprays can worsen their uneasy feelings. They could become increasingly stressed and bark more.

With permission, you can also do a little dog training yourself once you have met the Sheltie and it's clear the dog likes you. When there's a break in the Sheltie's barking, go to the fence with some healthy treats. (Ask the neighbors first if their dog has any food allergies.) Let the Sheltie see and smell the treats. When he is not barking, say *quiet* and give a treat. Walk away for a few seconds and come back. When he starts barking, say *quiet* and wait for him to stop talking before giving him the treat. What you are doing is teaching the Sheltie that silence is golden, and delicious.

The goal here is cooperation. You don't want a neighborhood feud. But if all of these suggestions fail, then you may have to contact your local municipality about noise ordinances that could apply to barking dogs. I hope, however, that this strategy is employed only as a last resort. Good luck!

HIS BARK IS WORSE THAN HIS BITE

Some dogs bark a little and some dogs bark a lot. In alphabetical order, here are the top 10 breeds known for their gift of gab, according to the American Kennel Club.

Airedale	Miniature pinscher
Boston terrier	Norwegian elkhound
Chihuahua	Pekingese
French bulldog	Schnauzer
Irish setter	Shetland sheepdog

The top 10 hush-puppy breeds are:

Afghan hound	Cocker spaniel
Basenji	Greyhound
Boxer	Leonberger
Brittany spaniel	Newfoundland
Bull terrier	Saluki

Strider and Daisy, Territorial Terrors

WHEN THEY HEARD THE FRONT DOOR OPEN, Strider, a male Siberian Husky-mix, and Daisy, a female Labrador-mix, immediately went into seek-and-destroy mode, sometimes lunging and growling at guests. Passersby felt threatened whenever Strider was outside because he would charge the fence, baring his teeth and growling. The mailman complained about delivering the mail. When owners Marcia and Pat had to stop inviting friends and family to visit, they realized they had a serious issue.

It was clear that Strider was the main problem. He went ballistic when a person or dog passed by their home, and Daisy backed him up. Strider vomited every day, licked himself and his bedding excessively, urine-marked in the house, growled at Pat, and slammed his whole body against the door if he heard a noise outside, even if the noise was his owners coming home from work.

A previous trainer's work with a shock collar was ineffective, since it did not address Strider's agitated, emotional state. All he learned was to stop barking when the collar was on. Once it came off, he resumed the outward displays of his true emotion: anxiety. Since urine-marking, vomiting, compulsive licking, and aggression can be signs of stress and anxiety, Strider was put on an antianxiety medication by his veterinarian. The medication helped reduce these behaviors, but didn't completely eliminate them.

We also took steps to make the house safer for everyone. The mailbox was moved from the house to the street. To stop their protective barking, the dogs were no longer permitted to be in the backyard unsupervised. Both dogs were trained to come when called and not to patrol the fence.

They were enrolled in a class designed for dogs who are uncomfortable around other dogs. We worked on changing Strider's emotional state when he was around people and other dogs from *must attack* to *nice to see you.* As he relaxed, we taught him coping behaviors for stressful situations. Instead of lunging and barking when the doorbell rings, Strider now runs to his mat in the kitchen and calmly looks to Marcia for advice on what to do.

Marcia and Pat have resumed hosting dinner parties and cookouts at their home. The dogs no longer lunge and bark at visitors or passersby. Strider's anxiety behaviors have also abated. While they still exercise caution when their dogs are around other people, Marcia and Pat can see that Strider and Daisy are more relaxed now that they understand that the humans decide whether the person at the front door is friend or foe.

Contributed by Pia Silvani, CPDT

Why All the Whining?

Q I recently adopted Gracie, a four-year-old mixed breed from my local animal shelter. I'm guessing that she is German shepherd, golden retriever, and perhaps collie. She was found as a stray and was a little underweight. I wanted an adult dog and adopted her because of her gentle, sweet nature. I have had dogs all my life, but Gracie ranks as the whiniest critter I've ever met. She shadows me around the house and whines all the time. She nudges me. She seems hungry for constant attention. Even when we return from long walks, she whines. I tell her everything is okay. I hug her. Still, she whines. What can I do to curb this whining? I love her very much, but she is driving me crazy!

A Like other canine sounds, whining is unmistakable. Bottom line: dogs whine to seek care. But there are many variations of the canine whine. Pups discover that by whining when they are cold or hungry, they attract their mother's attention. By the time these pups are old enough to be adopted, they have become very wise about whining. They transfer this whine-for-care behavior onto their new people parents. Some adult dogs also whine for attention. Others whine out of excitement, such as when they eye a squirrel through the kitchen window. Some whine due to pain or illness. Some whine out of frustration, especially when their favorite toy ball gets lodged under the sofa.

Even though Gracie's puppyhood and early adult years remain a mystery, you have the opportunity to develop a new relationship with her, preferably a whine-free one. First, have Gracie thoroughly examined by your veterinarian to rule out any possible medical reasons for her whining. If she is deemed to be physically fit, then you can work on changing her behavior. The goal is to communicate that she has a safe, caring home. The trick is to give Gracie love and attention without inadvertently reinforcing her whining ways. If you cater to her every whimper, you risk creating a very pushy, overly dependent dog who expects you to cater to her every need when she vocalizes or nudges.

One way to reduce whining is to provide Gracie with plenty of exercise each day. Take her on walks lasting at least 20 minutes. Play with her in the backyard. At home when she starts whining, try to figure out the reason. Respond to the legitimate ones, like the need to go outside or a reminder that it's dinnertime. But if she whines for the sake of whining, walk away. Ignore her. Really give her the cold shoulder. That means do not talk to her, look at her, or touch her. When she is quiet and calm, approach her, praise her calmly, and give her a treat.

You need to break the whining cycle, just like parents must do with fussy toddlers. If you don't nip this habit soon, it could develop into a full-blown case of separation anxiety. Once Gracie learns that whining gets her no attention from you, which is the opposite of what she desires, she will realize that being quiet reaps the best rewards.

Touchy Toes

Q I adopted a Welsh Corgi from a rescue group a couple of months ago. Booker is about 18 months old and from what I understand was neglected a lot as a puppy. His previous family said they were too busy to keep him. He is still adjusting to my home and acts timid and tentative.

I've taken steps to make him feel at home with a new doggy bed, treats, and lots of toys. He enjoys being petted, but he doesn't like his toes touched. He quickly pulls his paw from my grasp and tries to retreat. I know I need to keep his nails trimmed, but how can I convince him that I won't hurt his paws?

A First, thank you for giving Booker a second chance and a much better home. You're right. He is still adjusting to this new scene and has to build up his confidence and his trust in you. Second, many dogs of all breeds and mixes are fussy about having their toes touched, but corgis tend to be among the most toe shy, for reasons that remain mysterious. Several years ago, when I adopted Jazz, a corgi puppy, knowledgeable corgi breeders and trainers alerted me to this touchy toe trait and encouraged me to play with my puppy's toes from day one. Even though Booker is 18 months old, you can still train him to accept paw or toe touching. He may never welcome having his feet handled, but he can learn to tolerate it.

Even though dogs sport very tough paw pads, similar to thick leather soles on shoes, the rest of their foot anatomy was not designed to be as durable. The area on top and between the toes is especially sensitive to the touch for all dogs, not just corgis, because the area around the toes is packed with nerve endings that alert the brain to any pressure that could possibly cause pain or injury.

In Booker's case, in addition to his breed tendency, it is unlikely that anyone ever handled his paws, given his history. He may also harbor painful memories of bad pedicures. His nails may have been cut too short, causing bleeding and pain. If so, he will be vigilant in trying to protect his toes from future harm.

But as you mention, all dogs need trimmed nails. Overgrown nails can snag on carpet, scratch bare arms and legs, and affect the way a dog walks. The trick is to make toe touching a pleasant experience for Booker. To build his trust, start by teaching him to lift his front paw and touch your outstretched hand (hold a treat in your closed fist to encourage him) while you tell him *shake paws*. Don't grasp his paw at first; just touch it lightly and let it go. Heap on the praise and the treats. Slowly work up to holding his paw gently for a few seconds and releasing it before he struggles to escape. Once he is comfortable, ask him to shake with his other front paw. Keep sessions brief and remember the treats and praise, because you are helping to build new, happy memories in Booker.

You're ready for phase two. When Booker is resting quietly, lightly touch one paw and give it a gentle squeeze. Watch Booker's reaction. If he seems okay, bring out your happy voice and a treat. Proceed with touching a second paw, followed by praise and treats. I recommend that you also give him therapeutic massages that include touching his feet. If he is relaxed from a massage, he should be more tolerant of having you touch his feet.

Phase three calls for bringing out the nail clippers. Leave them in a favorite place, like on the sofa where the two of you hang out or next to his food bowl. When he sniffs the clippers, praise and hand out a treat. The goal is to get Booker to start viewing the nail clippers as another part of the household furnishings. Progress to sitting on the sofa with the clippers and a treat in your closed hand. Invite Booker to come up and sniff your hand. Open it slowly, show the clippers, and hand over the treat. When Booker stays, begin squeezing the clippers and tossing treats to get him to associate the sound with a tasty payday.

After a few weeks, begin clipping one paw at a time at first. Give him a special treat (hot dogs or cheese really motivate most dogs!) after each toe. Then stop the grooming session. Do the next paw the next day. Don't forget the treats. Gradually, you should be able to give Booker a full pedicure in one session.

No More Nipping

Q After my husband of 59 years died, I decided to adopt a puppy. Buddy fills my house with joy and happiness. He gives me companionship and makes me laugh. I also feel safer having him here, especially at night. Unfortunately, Buddy likes to nip my hands and arms to get my attention. He isn't biting aggressively, but his playful nips cause bruises and occasionally his teeth break the skin. My hands and arms are sore. I tried spraying Bitter Apple on my hands and arms, but Buddy actually likes the taste! What can I do to stop him from being so mouthy?

A Sounds like you have one spirited and loyal puppy. Mouthing is a very common behavior for puppies, who have very sharp baby teeth that are falling out to make room for adult teeth. Depending on the breed, this teething period and the desperate need to chew to soothe sore gums can last up to a year. I'm not sure what type of dog Buddy is, but a lot of herding dogs, such as Border collies, tend to use their mouths when they're playing. They have been bred to herd cattle and sheep by nipping at their heels. Some hunting dogs, like Labrador retrievers, are also particularly mouthy.

Whatever breed he is, the nipping and mouthing is still painful. Bitter Apple spray is usually effective because most dogs can't stand the taste. But there are always exceptions

like your Buddy. An effective alternative is breath freshener spray. The minty taste is far from being a canine favorite. You might also try dabbing your hands and arms with pickle juice. The juice contains a very sour additive called alum, which keeps the pickles crisp but is also a good dog deterrent, if you can stand the smell yourself!

It is more important, however, to train Buddy not to nip than to rely on repellents. He is bonding with you and needs to know that his nipping hurts. Around eight to ten weeks of age, puppies in litters learn about bite inhibition. When one puppy bites too hard, and his sibling yelps, he learns to soften his play bite. So when Buddy mouths you too roughly, you need to yelp loudly. In addition, you need to stand up, turn your back on him, and walk slowly away. The message is, "You are not fun right now, and playtime is over." Buddy wants to play with you and when you walk away, he will learn that mouthing ends good times.

That said, Buddy is at an age when he *needs* to chew. When he gets in a mouthy mood, offer him some suitable chew toys as substitutes for your hands and arms. When you play with him, use thick rope toys or rubber tugs that provide something safe for Buddy to put his mouth around while protecting your hands and arms. Please resist smacking his muzzle or holding his mouth closed, as these punitive tactics can backfire and cause him to bite more, and harder.

Talking to Deaf Dogs

Q When my Dalmatian died at age 14, I contacted a Dalmatian rescue group. I wanted to adopt an adult dog rather than raise a puppy again. I fell in love with two-year-old Gus, who is deaf. How can I teach him to listen to me when he can't hear my words? He wants to please but sometimes gets so distracted during walks that he doesn't pay attention to me. He is focused on a squirrel scurrying up a tree or hunting for cats hiding under cars. How can I communicate with him effectively?

A I applaud you for adopting Gus. No dog is perfect, even those with keen hearing. In the past, far too many good dogs were euthanized simply because they were deaf, whether due to a genetic disorder or injury. Dalmatians, Samoyeds, West Highland terriers, and white German shepherds are other breeds that show an increased risk for bilateral deafness, which is hearing loss that affects both ears.

When it comes to training deaf dogs, first realize that no dog speaks English and that most dogs get distracted by squirrels and cats! Dogs "talk" to each other primarily with nonverbal body language cues. Any noise they make, be it barking, yipping, whining, or growling, is secondary to their unspoken communication through sniffing, facial expression, and posturing. Second, recognize that just like hearing dogs, deaf dogs learn through consistency and patience. Instead of given spoken cues to Gus, you need to use sign language. Believe it or not, many people with deaf dogs have learned American Sign Language (ASL) in order to "speak" to their dogs. The added bonus is that you can now communicate with people with hearing loss as well.

You can also create your own hand signals to communicate with Gus. You need to choose gestures that are distinctly individualized to avoid confusion. You don't want your hand signal for *sit* to be too similar to your gesture for *come*. You need Gus's full attention to teach him any command. I recommend that you conduct your training sessions in a place with few distractions, such as your living

---

ASL SIGNS FOR COMMANDS

To learn more about training deaf dogs and to get specific step-by-step instructions on hand signals, visit the Deaf Dog Education Action Fund's Web site at www.deafdogs.org.

room, and at an optimum time, like right before mealtime when he is hungry. Catch his eye by thumping on the floor or waving your hand. One of the first commands you need to teach Gus is the *watch me* signal. While standing in front of Gus, take a small treat, bring it to his nose, then move the treat up to your eye. When Gus follows the movement of the treat, clap or give a thumbs-up approval sign and then hand him the treat. When Gus responds to *watch me* consistently, you are ready to introduce other signs.

When Gus masters a sign, give him a treat and use a consistent success signal like a thumbs-up or clap. Smile. Gus is looking for visual signals. Use treats and progress slowly. Build on each success and practice patience. Even deaf dogs are capable of learning dozens of signs and recognizing the difference in your request for a ball or the leash. In my dog agility class, it was weeks before I realized that one of my classmates had a deaf Sheltie named Alva. I just thought that Dale was a quiet, soft-spoken person! But Alva heeds Dale's hand signals and weaves through poles and dashes through tunnels with unspoken delight.

One word of caution with deaf dogs. Please keep Gus on a leash whenever you are walking or traveling and limit his off-leash play to areas that are safely fenced in. As an added safety measure, indicate on his tag that he is deaf and provide your name and contact information. A microchip is another good way to help you find Gus if he ever becomes lost.

DOGGY HAND SIGNALS

Many handlers who compete in obedience and field trials teach their dogs to respond to hand signals instead of voice cues. While any signal that makes sense to you is acceptable, here are some that are commonly used. All of these assume that your dog is facing you.

COME. Start with your arm straight out to the side at shoulder height. Sweep your arm energetically across your chest, bringing your hand to your opposite shoulder.

SIT. Start with your arm at your side, palm facing forward. Bend your elbow to bring your hand up to your shoulder.

DOWN. Start with your arm straight out in front of you at shoulder height with palm facing down. Keeping your elbow straight, bring your arm down toward your hip.

STAY. Put your straight arm in front of your dog's nose, with your palm out like a traffic cop.

PART III

Why Does My Dog Do That?

Sometimes our dogs do wild and crazy things that puzzle us. We wonder why they can't just act more like, well, humans. It would make life so much easier if our dogs would greet people by extending their front paws for a hearty hello, or bypass the toilet and drink fresh water from their bowls, or resist the temptation to raid the cat's litter box for a late-night snack.

Face the Fido facts. Dogs will be dogs. If they could express themselves in words, dogs would probably admit that they are equally puzzled by our behavior. Why, for example, do people fail to sniff others during introductions? Why do people forget to utter at least one "I mean business" bark when a delivery guy dares to ring the doorbell? And, come on, people, there's a dead fish marinating nicely on the sandy beach — why aren't you rolling in it?

Don't worry. By the time you finish this section, you will possess so much more dog sense that your favorite canine pal might even come up and congratulate you with a big sloppy kiss or a quick sniff of your rear end.

Marathon Barker

Q How can I get my beagle, Jake, to stop barking whenever someone rings my doorbell, knocks on my front door, or walks past my house? A few barks are okay, but Jake barks on and on and at a volume so high that I want to take out my hearing aid so I don't have to hear his noise. When I yell at him to stop, he ignores me and barks even louder.

A Some types of dogs are born barkers. The hound breeds, like Jake and his cousins the basset hounds, foxhounds, and bloodhounds, were bred to use their bark to communicate with their owners during hunts. In addition to their breed histories, some dogs are very territorial. In their minds, your home is their domain to defend. Jake is sounding the alarm and if we could translate his barks, he is probably saying, "Come quick! Check it out! Friend or foe? What do you want me to do? Now you're yelling, too, so I'd better keep barking!"

As you can see, yelling at Jake to stop barking is futile, because barking dogs interpret our loud vocalizations as our attempt to join in the warning. Your yelling has unintentionally served to reinforce his yapping. You will need to re-train Jake so that he develops a new association with the sound of your doorbell. Start by ringing your doorbell. When Jake barks, ignore him. Patiently wait for him to stop. After a few seconds of silence, introduce a cue by

SNIFF IT OUT!

Dogs may not chuckle, but they do show amusement. Instead of giggles, they display a distinct rapid panting to convey pleasure and playfulness. Look for it the next time you play a game of fetch. And many people swear that their dogs smile.

saying *hush* and then reward him. Timing is critical — do not reward him until he has been quiet for several seconds. Think like a dog for a moment. If given the options, which would you choose: keep barking or hush and garner a tasty prize?

Conduct these training sessions several times a day until Jake figures out that *hush* means to be quiet and that being quiet brings treats, while barking brings nothing. Make the pauses between his silence and your *hush* cue longer and longer. Then start saying *hush* when he is actually barking and reward him when he stops. Remember not to keep repeating that phrase, though, because it will only reinforce Jake to continue barking.

I also have a backup training strategy: diversion. Instead of yelling at Jake when he barks at a passerby, call him to you and reward him for performing a desired behavior, like sitting in front of you for a moment or fetching his favorite toy. For safety reasons, you don't want Jake to behave like a canine mime when someone approaches your home. It is good that he alerts you, but by trying diversionary tactics and rewarding his silences rather than his noise, you will benefit by having a better-behaved Jake who no longer irritates your ears with nonstop yapping.

Why the Fuss over the FedEx Guy?

Q The postal carrier comes to my house every afternoon and places mail through the slot in my front door. His arrival sets off my dog, who goes ballistic barking and lunging at the front door. Grange also launches into a barking barrage when a delivery person rings my doorbell. I'm not winning any popularity contests with my mailman or delivery people. What can I do to get Grange to calm down?

A Don't you wish that you could just have a person-to-dog chat with Grange and explain the deal about delivery people? Unfortunately, he is abiding by a well-known doggy formula: Dog hears or sees someone in a uniform approach the front door. Dog sounds an alert to the leader of his pack (that's you) and barks aggressively at the intruder. The intruder then retreats, leaving the dog to believe that he has successfully stopped another home invasion. The score is always Dog 1, Uniform 0 in this daily delivery game. Grange may bark out of a need to protect or out of fear or excitement, depending on his personality type, but each time this scenario occurs it cements his belief that his actions are working.

It is vital to ensure the safety of these folks in uniform. National statistics indicate that dogs bite about 3,000 postal carriers each year. For starters, there are a couple of things *not* to do when a delivery person arrives at your front porch. When Grange barks, do not say things like "it's okay" or "good boy," because that actually rewards him for barking. In his mind, he thinks that you are agreeing with his need to be a ferocious barking machine. At the same time, don't yell at him to shut up — he'll just think you are helping him warn off the intruder.

Here are some things you *can* do. First, see the previous question about teaching a barker how to *hush*. You also mentioned that you have a mail slot in your front door. That slot can deliver not only mail but also doggy treats. See if your postal carrier and other delivery people are willing to put treats through the slot. You can keep a sealed container of treats outside your door. The idea is to get Grange to anticipate good things when the uniformed people approach. (Sure beats junk mail!)

This technique is known as counterconditioning. You are striving to replace a bad association with a good one. If you happen to spot the mail carrier or delivery person coming up the street, you can implement a barking prevention plan. Sprinkle treats on the floor in front of your door for Grange to eat while deliveries are being

made. Timing is important. You must present the treats before he makes his first bark. He cannot be madly barking while gobbling a shower of treats. It's impossible for these two actions to occur at the same time.

Another strategy requires you to clearly step into the role of household commander so that Grange realizes when a uniformed person approaches, you will be the one who calls the shots. During this training time, you may need to fit Grange with a head halter or other tool that provides control without pain. When the uniformed person approaches, teach Grange to *sit* and *stay* while you hold the leash to accept the package in your doorway. Reward him with treats each time he complies. If you are not confident about how to put on a head halter, then seek help from your veterinarian or local dog trainer.

Instilling proper greeting behavior from the time a dog is first brought home should prevent any barking, snapping, or lunging habits from ever developing. When I brought home my first puppy, I would carry him to the door to meet and greet my delivery people. They would give him a treat and a couple more when he learned to sit on cue. As he grew up, Jazz learned that the person in uniform is like a canine Santa Claus and would happily join me at the front door. He would then plop into a *sit* and wait for his reward without a single bark.

===

Champion Crotch Sniffer

Q This is a bit embarrassing, but I need your help. My otherwise polite Great Dane, Dolly, loves to greet people. Unfortunately, her style of greeting often includes rushing up to guests and sticking her nose in their crotches. Dolly is a big dog and it is difficult for me to yank her back. She is good about not jumping up on people, but some of my friends are offended by her preferred method of greeting. What can I do to stop this obnoxious behavior?

A Dolly is 100 percent dog. When dogs meet and greet each other, it is very common for them to sniff each other thoroughly from head to tail. The canine nose gives the "sniffer" a lot of details about the "sniffee" (age, health condition, what they ate for breakfast, and even their moods). They aim for the rear end because the scents are more intense there than other places on the body.

Dogs like Dolly need to learn that this doggy greeting is not well received by the two-legged crowd. Large breeds like Great Danes are generally the biggest offenders, because their noses are at just the right level to poke someone between the legs. It is not uncommon for them to do a front *and* a back sniff. Tiny breeds like Chihuahuas and Yorkshire terriers are more apt to be fascinated by a newcomer's shoes or ankles, because that's as high as they can reach.

Please don't be too embarrassed. Plenty of dogs are guilty of this "crime," and people shouldn't get too huffy and offended by what is perfectly polite canine etiquette. You can teach Dolly to be a more acceptable greeter, however. The goal is to show her the preferred way to say hello while making it worth her while to change her behavior. The first step is to make sure she has a good grounding in basic obedience. All dogs, but especially giant ones like Dolly, need to be able to *sit* and *stay* when told. Reinforce those commands when the house is quiet and then have her *sit* and *stay* when a guest comes in the door. Ask your guests to approach Dolly first, rather than letting Dolly take the initiative.

Some dogs are very expressive with their front legs. If that is the case with Dolly, you can teach her to swap sniffing for paw shaking. Start by working with her by yourself. Ask her to *sit*. Hold out a treat in your hand positioned just below her nose. Most dogs will paw at the treat. When Dolly does this, grab her raised paw, shake it in a friendly way, say *good shake* or *good paw,* and then hand over the treat. Give her plenty of praise for a job well done.

Once Dolly is shaking paws consistently, invite friends to give her the *good shake* cue. If Dolly slips back to her old routine, ask the guest to simply turn around and walk a few paces away and ignore Dolly. She will soon learn that sniffing doesn't yield her the goodies that sitting politely to shake paws does. Work on extending the time Dolly stays in a sit, too.

Finally, expand your horizon by practicing this greeting with Dolly when you are outside the home. Do it when friends approach you on the sidewalk during dog walks or when you are in the parking lot of your supermarket. The goal is to expose Dolly to a lot of situations so she learns this is an acceptable greeting for people, as long as they initiate the contact.

In extreme cases, you may need to rely on a spray bottle containing a mixture of vinegar and water or mint breath spray. Keep this spray near your door. When Dolly prepares to plunge her nose into a person's crotch, take aim and spray her in the face (but please, avoid her eyes). The spray smells unpleasant to most dogs. This is a form of aversion therapy and is designed to create a negative experience. A few times seeing the spray bottle and your dog will quickly connect the dots and back off. I only advise this in situations involving very pushy canine greeters and I add this caution with using this type of punishment approach: cease the spray bottle approach if your dog shows any tendency to attack the spray bottle or to act aggressively at the sight of it. You don't want your training to backfire and create a worse problem.

Making a Splash

Q I swear that my dog, Jesse, is part duck. He loves to splash water out of his bowl with his front paws. He creates a big mess all over the kitchen floor. The bowl is empty and I keep refilling it, only to have Jesse paw out the water again. What's going on?

A Jesse is certainly making a big splash — of the undesired kind. You shouldn't need rubber boots to wade through your kitchen! I'm not sure what breed Jesse is, but he's probably a water-loving breed like a Labrador retriever. These dogs are drawn to swimming and playing in water (and doing the full-body shake afterward).

Every dog-occupied home needs bowls of fresh, clean water to keep canines hydrated. I can see how tricky that can be in your home, but there are several approaches to resolve this watery mess. First, the ever-growing population of pet owners has created a big industry of new pet products. You can purchase water bowls in all shapes, sizes, and structures at pet supply stores and online. If Jesse is actually knocking over his bowl, you might consider one with a nonskid bottom. A bowl that sits off the ground on a platform might thwart his splashing efforts. You might also consider water feeder bottles that require dogs to lick at the tip to release a small flow of water (similar to those found in rabbit cages).

Another strategy is to monitor your dog's water intake rather than leave water down for him at all times. Present the water bowl half-filled after Jesse comes in from a walk or other type of exercise and after meals. Hold the bowl down and let Jesse drink. If he starts to put his front paws into the bowl, pick it up. Wait for him to sit or become calm and then put the water bowl back down again. You are trying to convey to Jesse that his water bowl is not a source of play but only for quenching thirst. If you opt for this method, be sure you offer him water numerous times throughout the day, especially during hot weather.

Good luck with Jesse and be sure to keep plenty of paper towels and a mop handy during this transitional time.

COME ON IN — THE WATER'S FINE!

If you have a water-loving dog, offer him a suitable outlet to make a splash. Buy a small plastic wading pool for your backyard or patio. Fill it about halfway with water and let your dog romp and splash outdoors to his heart's content. Reward him with treats and praise.

Lavatory Lapping

Q I keep several water bowls around my house and always dutifully keep them filled with clean, fresh water. But Jules, my boxer, prefers lapping water out of the toilet bowl, which I find disgusting! Why does he do that? Will he get sick?

A Disgusting is a good description for this common doggy deed. But it makes sense if you think like a dog, not a civilized person who craves bottled or carbonated water with a fancy name. To a thirsty canine, the toilet simply provides a giant porcelain oasis of fresh, cool water in a huge bowl that never moves or tips over and is always full. And don't forget about location. Bathrooms often feature tile floors that sooth canine pads on hot days. As far as Jules is concerned, the toilet is your home's Number One water bowl.

As for germs, even if you pride yourself on keeping the cleanest bathroom in your block, your dog isn't wowed by that fact. There is a slight risk that your dog can get sick if you pour lots of cleaning chemicals in your toilet, but in general the water in your toilet bowl is actually cleaner — and safer — than most puddles, lakes, and ponds. It's an unfortunate fact that these public bodies of water often harbor nasty germs and parasites that can cause giardia and other illnesses in our dogs.

Another reason Jules may head to the bathroom instead of his water bowls could be the bowl itself. Plastic bowls absorb odors and may cause the water to taste off, even to a dog. Consider switching to ceramic or stainless steel water bowls that can be easily cleaned in the dishwasher.

The simplest solution to this problem is to keep the lid down. I know that it's easier said than done; we often forget or visitors inadvertently leave it up. You can put up a sign for guests saying *Please keep the lid down to keep Jules from drinking,* but that won't enhance your home décor. You may decide to keep your bathroom door closed.

A final tip: Water bowls kept in sunny places can be doggy turnoffs. Make sure that water bowls are in spots where they will keep cool. Heighten their appeal by tossing in a few ice cubes to provide a welcoming chill on particularly warm days.

Doing the Dead Fish Dance

Q My one-year-old foxhound is in constant search of different smells and always has his nose to the ground. I recognize that is the nature of being a scent breed, but Clyde doesn't just stop at sniffing. Whenever he discovers something rotting and disgusting like a dead frog or fish on the beach or his favorite, road kill, he takes great delight in flopping down and rolling all over it. He smells terrible afterward. Why on earth does he do this?

A No one really knows why dogs roll in smelly stuff, but there are several theories. One is that this is an instinctive behavior harkening back to pre-domesticated days when hunting dogs would bring back information about available food to the rest of the packs. The thought was, if they found decaying fish, perhaps fresher fish could be found nearby. Some modern-day dogs may have retained this behavior even though it has lost its once-necessary function.

A second theory is that dogs roll in foul-smelling material to provide an olfactory disguise to improve their hunting opportunities. What better way to catch a rabbit, say, than to smell like one, even a dead one, rather than like a dog? This canine camouflage technique also may be employed to hide their doggy scents from other predators.

Unfortunately, dogs and owners will never agree on what smells nice and what smells disgusting. Owners carefully shampoo their dogs, rinse them, towel them dry, and brush them. To them, the dog is finally clean and smelling sweet. To the dog, however, the shampoo is a dreadful stench that needs to be disguised immediately. That explains why many freshly bathed dogs will dash outside and roll in the dirt. Some even prefer to roll in poop to cover that awful shampoo smell. It's their version of a high-priced perfume or cologne.

SNIFF IT OUT!
Dogs possess about 20 times more scent-receptor cells than humans. They can use their noses to sniff out odors that contain only a few parts per billion.

When you are on walks with Clyde, keep him within sight so that you can spot him the minute he dives on a "stink bomb" and distract him from it. If he's found something gross in a particular area, avoid that spot for a few days or leash him until you are safely beyond temptation. Always carry treats with you so that you can call him back to you when he seems too interested in something disgusting. Reinforce the *leave it* command, so you stand a greater chance of stopping him before he can roll in the smelly find. (See Ignoring Temptation, page 169.) For people with dogs who roll in droppings, I recommend stepping up the poop patrol in the backyard to remove that particular temptation.

Raider of the Litter Box

Q I enjoy cats and dogs, which explains why my home includes both. But I can't seem to keep my dog from eating feces from the litter box. What's the attraction and how can I end Sassy's disgusting raids on the litter box?

A You can impress your friends and expand your vocabulary by being able to speak of this behavior by its scientific name: coprophagy (stool eating). The fact that there is a fancy name for this act tells you that Sassy isn't the only canine with this fetish, which is shared by many members of the animal kingdom. Many dogs eat the stools of other animals (rabbits, deer, and horses) and some even nibble on their own deposits.

This habit could signal a vitamin deficiency in your dog's diet, so please consult your veterinarian if you suspect that nutrition is involved. Your dog may need to switch to a new diet that is higher in protein, fiber, or fat, or she may need vitamin B supplements. However, there are other reasons that Sassy indulges in such a revolting habit. When taking care of their litters, Sassy's ancestors learned to ingest stools to keep their dens clean and be less likely to draw the attention of predators. Nursing bitches still clean up their whelping boxes this way when their young puppies are first born.

A second explanation is a matter of taste. Humans find the idea repulsive, but dogs are omnivores (they eat meat and veggies) and their palate differs greatly from ours. Litter box stools probably taste of cat food, which most dogs eat happily.

A third reason is that Sassy might be bored and raiding the litter box just to add some zip to her otherwise mundane day. If this is the case, make sure she has two or more regular daily walks of at least 20 minutes so that she uses up some of that extra energy. Spending a few minutes a day teaching her tricks can counter boredom as well. When you leave her alone, provide a distraction to the lure of the litter box by giving her a rawhide bone or a hollow toy stuffed with treats.

Whatever the reason, this problem can be conquered. Cats like to have their private places — dog-free zones, if you will. In my own home, I've placed the litter boxes in a spare bedroom and blocked access to my dog with a gate at the doorway. The gate is positioned above the floor just enough to allow the cats to slide under or leap over the top, giving them two ways to enter and exit the room. I also keep their food bowls in there, so Chipper can't snack out of those, either.

I've trained Chipper to sit and stay when I enter and exit the cat room. Her politeness is rewarded each morning when I give the cats a dollop of canned food. When I leave, Chipper is patiently awaiting her own dollop, having learned that staying outside this room is worth her while.

Blocking access works until you forget to shut the doggy gate to the cat room. As a final remedy, I also recommend that you step up your "poop patrol" and clean the litter boxes more frequently. Since it can be hard to be vigilant, you might sprinkle some pancreatic enzymes (available at pet supply stores or health stores) on the litter to make the stool taste anything but doggone great to Sassy. This works only if your cats appear to be unbothered by this addition to their litter box and continue using it. You don't want a sudden litter box boycott by your cats!

Tennis, Anyone?

Q Every morning when I wake up, I can guarantee there will be a smelly, dirty tennis ball on my pillow. If I ignore that ball, I get a wet, cold nose in my face and lots of doggy kisses from Nelly, my year-old yellow Lab. She is a ball nut. When I take her to the local dog park, she ignores all the other dogs and just focuses on fetching ball after ball. I have to end the game after a half-hour because I'm afraid she will run herself to sheer exhaustion. Why is she so consumed with chasing a ball all the time?

A Ah, the art and obsession of the ball chase. I see a lot of dogs fitting Nelly's actions at the various dog parks in my area. They only have eyes for their favorite toy. When they do come in contact with another dog, they give a quick greeting and go right back to their ball. Some dogs also seem to know which people are the easy marks with the best arms and will use their canine charm to persuade other people to throw the ball when their owner gets tired.

If you think about canine ancestry, chasing balls isn't that different from chasing rabbits and other small prey.

Dogs were the original eat-on-the-run types. The chase brought them a positive prize — food and a full belly. Today, our pampered pooches don't have to pursue their meals, but that "chase and catch" instinct is still wired into the genes of many breeds, particularly the hunting breeds like retrievers and spaniels. Though most family dogs no longer hunt with their owners, they find that spongy, spit-saturated tennis ball as satisfying as a downed duck would be. In contrast, you won't find many Shih Tzus or Akitas begging for marathon ball-tossing sessions. It's just not in their breed history.

Obviously, Nelly is getting plenty of exercise, but it appears that she has crossed the line from being fit to becoming fanatical. The morning ritual also signals to me that Nelly views herself as the one calling the shots — the minute you wake up, she is forcing you to pay attention to her. She is young, but you don't want to run the risk of her developing into a ball bully. Since you know that the tennis ball motivates Nelly, use it to your advantage in establishing yourself firmly as leader. For starters, put all tennis balls and other similar temptations away at bedtime. Some people stash all balls and Frisbees outside and don't allow any indoor ball play at all.

Bring out the tennis ball only when you decide it is time to play fetch. With each throw, reinforce Nelly's manners by having her *sit* and *stay* for a few seconds or more before you toss the ball again. Use this time to teach Nelly the *drop it* and *leave it* cues. If she doesn't want to drop or leave the ball, bring out a second ball and offer to throw it if she drops the first one. Work on your recall as well, so that she is paying attention to you and not just the ball during your play sessions.

On those occasions when there are dogs at the dog park who aren't chasing balls, see if you can work on Nelly's

PAW PRINTS

The name of the dog on the Cracker Jack box is Bingo. The dog in the famous RCA ad is Nipper. The dog who accompanies Buster Brown is named Tige; the pair were well-known cartoon characters before their images were purchased by the shoe company.

dog-to-dog social skills by stashing her toys in a bag out of sight temporarily and encouraging her to play some doggy games instead. Or, invite a couple of friends with friendly canines over to your backyard or basement for playtime without any toys, especially balls.

I applaud you for knowing when enough is enough and ending the ball-throwing game. Dogs can run themselves into exhaustion by not knowing when to quit, especially in hot weather. Please be sure to provide Nelly with plenty of water afterward. I recommend always keeping a water bottle and a plastic bowl in the car in case the water at the dog park is dirty or your dog doesn't realize she is thirsty until you are back at the car.

Salad Days

Q My dog will occasionally eat grass and then vomit a few moments later. He seems fine and I don't detect any health problem. What's the deal with dogs and grass? I thought they were meat eaters.

A Dogs like a little variety in their diet and know the value of adding some greens to the menu. They are actually omnivores, which means they eat meat and vegetation — not to mention kibble from any available cat bowl (feline food always seems to have a more beckoning aroma), table scraps in your kitchen garbage can (if you forget to put on the lid), and all sorts of other things at which humans turn up their noses.

Some dogs frequently eat grass and don't throw up afterward. They may simply like the taste and feel the need to add some roughage to their regular meals. This pertains more to those dogs who actually chew and swallow the grass blades thoroughly. Grass can also act as a healthful aid for dogs with upset stomachs who need to purge their systems. In that case, you might notice that they seem to almost gobble the grass without really chewing the blades. The prickly little stalks irritate their stomach linings and cause them to vomit. That sounds like the case with your dog. If this occurs only occasionally, let nature take its course. But if he is vomiting daily and isn't eating well, please consult your veterinarian. There may be an underlying medical reason behind this behavior.

Grass is fine for dogs when it is free of pesticides, lawn chemicals, or other harmful substances. I recommend that you grow a container of grass for your dog to nibble on indoors or provide him with a patch of special greens in your backyard. You will be offering food that offers certain vitamins, minerals, and fiber not found in the meat in his food bowl. And don't forget to entice his taste buds by adding some cooked or raw vegetables, such as green beans or carrots, to his food bowl.

Threatened by Thunder

Q I live in Indiana, where we have nasty thunderstorms that throw my dog into a four-legged panic. She whines and whimpers when the storms approach and then tries desperately to hide under my bed or in my bathtub. She shivers with fright. Why do thunderstorms cause this strong reaction?

A Sadly, your dog is not alone. Even before that first thunder boom or lightning flash, many dogs scurry into closets, crawl under beds, or leap into bathtubs. Some even try to dig through the carpet in a desperate attempt to hide, or crash through windows or doors to escape the terrifying noise. Fear of uncontrollable situations is a natural response in people and animals, but if fear worsens with repeated exposure to the stimuli, it can become a phobia. A phobia is defined as a fear that is out of proportion to the danger of the actual situation or event. There is nothing wrong with being afraid of walking on an icy sidewalk, for example, unless it causes you to stay inside all winter.

Without proper intervention, phobias escalate with repeated exposure to the stimulus. For dogs, phobias often involve loud noises, such as

BREED BYTE

Owners of basset hounds, bloodhounds, bullmastiffs, and Saint Bernards have learned to keep plenty of towels on hand. These lovable dogs are the sloppiest of breeds.

the sound of thunderstorms, the backfire from a car, or skateboard wheels scraping on pavement. Dogs have been known to physically harm themselves — and others — in their attempts to escape these frightening sounds.

The first step in dealing with a fearful or anxious dog is to schedule a complete physical examination with your veterinarian to rule out any possible underlying medical problem, such as hypothyroidism, Cushing's disease, or other condition. Anxiety-reducing medications can help some dogs with phobias, but it is also vital to reinforce basic obedience behaviors like *sit, down,* and *stay,* and to teach them to focus on an activity that distracts from the sound of the storm. Be sure to provide your pet with tasty treats during these training sessions.

Desensitization is often paired with counterconditioning. Desensitization uses baby steps to build your dog's confidence. If he is afraid of loud noises, you expose him to the sound at low volume and reward him for being calm. You can purchase CDs of storm sounds at music stores or online. As he continues to demonstrate no fear, you gradually increase the volume. Counterconditioning associates the presence of the trigger (an approaching storm, for instance) with a positive experience such as eating or playing. You can also teach your dog to *down stay* in his crate or on a mat or other safe place when there are no storms around. Once he learns this relaxation behavior, you can teach him to settle down in that safe place during a storm.

These techniques require patience and make take quite a bit of time, so don't expect an instant cure. Never punish a fearful pet by yelling or striking, because such actions can worsen his phobias and anxieties. Instead, touch your dog gently and speak calmly to reassure him but avoid excessive displays of concern or petting. Speak in upbeat tones, act happy, and divert your pet's attention to a treat or fun activity. Your goal is to deliver a message that the storm is no big deal.

Even with careful training, some pets need medications to conquer phobias. Some over-the-counter herbal or homeopathic remedies or pheromone diffusers may ease anxiety levels. For severe cases, however, antianxiety or antidepressant medications may be necessary. Work closely with your veterinarian in selecting and monitoring the effect these medications have on your dog. It is

SIGNS OF A TERRIFIED DOG

A dog with a phobia may display these behaviors:

Freezing in one place, refusing to move

Pacing frantically

Trembling and shaking

Hyper-salivating, lip-licking, and yawning

Attempting to flee or escape

Hiding

Eliminating inappropriately

Vocalizing by whining excessively

not uncommon for veterinarians to adjust the dosage or switch to a different medication when treating thunderstorm phobias. Be aware that some prescriptions must be given daily for up to one month before they are effective. Others work on an as-needed basis. The long-term goal is to eventually wean your dog from medications, although some dogs may need medications for their entire lives.

Rhett Overcomes Anxiety

RHETT, AN 18-MONTH-OLD neutered Norfolk terrier, appeared to be an ideal dog, but he had been behaving strangely for two months. His owner, Tanya, described him as unable to sit still and constantly "air licking" (a distinct behavior where a dog repetitively flicks its tongue in the air) and snapping at imaginary flies. These odd displays occurred on and off during the day but seemed worse in the early evening. Tanya could sometimes stop Rhett's behavior by bribing him with food, giving him a massage, or taking him for a walk, but his frantic activity was increasing, which prompted her to seek my help.

The major relevant fact in this case was that the family was in the process of moving. In some dogs, tail chasing and fly snapping have been associated with partial seizures. But in Rhett's case, the start of his odd behavior was clearly triggered by changes in the household due to the planned relocation. The sight of packing boxes seemed quite stressful for Rhett.

His anxiety also seemed to be caused in part by Rosie, the family's second Norfolk terrier, who was younger and had been adopted after Rhett. She pestered Rhett more than he liked during playtime and on walks. I noted that he was showing stress-related displacement behavior that had the potential to develop into compulsive behavior.

To start our multifaceted approach, Rhett was given a low dose of an antianxiety medication after his veterinarian ruled out any underlying medical causes. Tanya began to reinforce Rhett's place as the senior-ranking dog by ensuring that he was always ahead of Rosie when receiving meals, toys, and attention, and going outdoors. He also benefited from having time to play with his toys away from Rosie and from longer daily walks and other exercise.

When treating compulsive disorders, it is vital to either minimize exposure or desensitize the dog to the stressor that is triggering the behavior. Since the disruption of the move couldn't be avoided, Tanya diverted Rhett by hiding food in hollow dog toys and burying toys and treats in the backyard for him to discover by digging. This shifted his energy from compulsive flank licking and fly snapping to busily finding goodies. As just having everything boxed up and in disarray was stressful, we made the boxes fun by teaching him to jump on and off them, run the gauntlet, and find hidden treats among them.

After the move to the new home and the introduction of new canine ranking rules for Rhett and Rosie, Rhett's compulsive ways steadily subsided and his gentle, calm nature returned. This is a case where early intervention helped prevent the escalation of strange behaviors.

Contributed by Alice Moon-Fanelli, PhD

Dog Despises Dishwasher

Q When we're at work, we keep Sally, our 10-month-old Border collie, in our kitchen, which is gated to keep her from running around the house. For some reason, Sally hates our dishwasher. She barks at it when it's running. She lunges at the door handle when we try to open it. At first we laughed, but now her behavior is no joking matter. Why is she doing this and how can we keep her from destroying our appliance?

A I thought I had the only dishwasher-hating dog. My corgi Jazz had nothing but disdain for my dishwasher. Any attention paid to that appliance would cause him to bark, lunge, growl, and physically try to wrestle the handle (which looked pretty silly). My dishwasher had teeth marks on the door handle and scratches all over the front. Like Sally, Jazz was a herding dog. Herding breeds can be stubborn and determined; after all, they must dodge kicking cows and sheep while moving them from one place to the next. Herding dogs are also highly intelligent and energetic. These dogs need jobs, because boredom brings out their worst behaviors.

You need to give the dishwasher a new identity — one that is either boring or appealing to Sally, not annoying. One way to circumvent a quirky problem like this and prevent it from escalating into physical harm or a wider hatred of other noise-producing appliances is to limit exposure to the dishwasher. You mentioned that she is kept in your kitchen during the day. Perhaps you could put her in a different safe place in your home while you're away.

Everyone in your household needs to play by the same rules when it comes to the dishwasher. Since your kitchen is gated, put Sally on the other side of the gate when you load and unload the dishes. Perhaps someone in your house can distract her in another room or even play a game of fetch with her in the backyard while another person deals with the dishes. Or put her in her crate in a bedroom with music on to muffle the sound of the dishes. The idea is to limit her exposure to this "menacing" machine. While you are working on this problem, try to run the dishwasher only at night when she is safe inside your bedroom or her crate or at other times when Sally won't be in the kitchen. This may be impractical in the long run, however, so you might want to take the opposite approach and convince her that the dishwasher is not dangerous. The idea is to build a history of fun times associated with the appliance. A dog cannot be happy and angry at the same time. No one can.

If she is ball- or treat-motivated, start by having her sit and wait for the ball or treat in a room near the kitchen. Gradually, bring her closer and closer until she is sitting next to the dishwasher. Have her *sit* and *stay* while you touch the dishwasher. (Don't open it yet!) If she stays quiet, reward her with a treat or a minute of ball tossing. You may need to keep her on a leash at first so you can step on the leash to stop her if she attempts to attack the dishwasher. Slowly work your way up to opening the door a few inches at a time while rewarding her for sitting still.

When Sally consistently ignores the dishwasher and will sit or play fetch near it, increase the exposure a bit by placing premium treats on the opened lid of the dishwasher. Again, have Sally perform a trick before she is allowed to take these treats. Once she's comfortable with the silent dishwasher, try turning it on for a second or two, shutting it off, and rewarding her for behaving calmly. Add a few seconds at a time while continuing to reward proper behavior.

Remember, the biggest mistake people make is to try to go too quickly, which usually makes the problem worse. It may take days, weeks, or even months, but eventually Sally will build up enough memorable experiences involving treats and toys near the dishwasher that she will gain a new appreciation for this appliance.

Toy Tactics

Q When she's playing, my puppy crouches down, wiggles her body, and then leaps up in the air as if she has springs in her legs, landing on her favorite toys. She grabs them and shakes them back and forth, growling. It's comical to watch, but what is she doing?

A Your puppy is doing what comes naturally: She is practicing the age-old art of hunting and "killing" her prey. Okay, so the prey in this case happens to be a stuffed plush hamburger from the local pet store. Why ruin your puppy's fun?

Her leaping and pouncing represent scripted actions of the chase response and can be seen in wild canids all over the world as they hunt mice and other small animals in grass and snow. This behavior starts to surface in puppies by about five weeks of age. Coyote and fox pups imitate the stalking, pouncing, and killing actions of adults to learn vital skills. For domestic dogs, this behavior in puppies is still an important part of the physical and mental growth process of puppyhood. Unless your puppy becomes very aggressive or possessive over her toys, enjoy these leaping moments of pure puppy play.

Skateboard Shivers

Q I adopted my dog a few months ago, and my best guess is that she is a beagle-Labrador mix between two and three years old. Belle loves going to new places and exploring new sights, sounds, and smells. But for some reason, she is absolutely terrified of skateboards. She yanks the leash and tries desperately to flee the scene. What is going on and how can I help her be less afraid?

A If only our dogs could communicate in plain English about the reasons behind their fears. Clearly, Belle has some negative association with skateboards, but you'll never know exactly what it is. It may be as simple as the fact that the scraping sound irritates her ears, much like fingernails on a chalkboard send some students into spasms. More likely, she had a negative experience involving a skateboard when she was a puppy. The wheels could have rolled over her toes or she could have collided with a fast-moving skateboarder and been injured. Unfortunately, she might have been teased by kids on skateboards, although in that case you could expect her to be afraid of children as well.

Your best option is to work on a remedy. Keep your ears tuned on walks for the sound of a skateboard in the distance. Belle's ears are better than yours, so watch her for signs of nervousness and react promptly to get her attention. The goal is to try to intervene with a positive experience as the sound gets closer. Distract Belle by speaking to her in an upbeat tone and asking her to practice some of her favorite tricks like sitting up, shaking paws, or rolling over — all while on a leash for safety. Carry a pouch of doggy treats and dole them out as the skateboard goes by.

Another tactic is to borrow an old skateboard from a neighbor or friend or buy one at a garage sale. The strategy calls for you to gradually introduce the skateboard to Belle so that she gains a new association with these wheeled wonders. Put the skateboard in one room of your house, but don't roll it. Each time Belle walks by it or cautiously goes up to investigate it, toss her a treat.

As she becomes accustomed to the skateboard, try placing treats on it. Praise her when she takes these treats. Once Belle consistently approaches the skateboard without hesitation, place a few treats on the skateboard and slowly move it a few inches forward and backward. Do this on carpeting first to keep the wheels quiet. Encourage Belle to grab the treats while the skateboard is moving. When she shows no fear of indoor skateboards, go outdoors and gradually increase the movement and sound on your garage floor or driveway.

> **SNIFF IT OUT!**
> Dogs are not color-blind, as many people think. They cannot see color as vividly as we do, however, and due to the structure of the rod receptors in their eyes, they can see yellow tennis balls far more easily than red or green ones.

Finally, solicit the aid of a dog-friendly skateboarder. Ask your helper to walk up to Belle holding the skateboard in his hands. Have him give Belle treats for being brave enough to approach and check out the skateboard. Later, as Belle's confidence builds, ask him to roll the skateboard on the ground with his hand. Keep rewarding her at each stage.

The speed of your progress depends on your attention to Belle's responses. Never advance to the next level of exposure until Belle clearly demonstrates no fear at the current level. The more positive exposure Belle accumulates, the better the chance that she won't try to dodge and dash when a skateboard approaches on your walks.

Stares at Stairs

Q My dachshund, Danny, is a very confident fellow. He goes boldly up to larger dogs at the dog park and solicits them to play. He doesn't blink during thunderstorms and loves to greet visitors to my home. The problem is that I have recently moved to a condominium on the second floor with outside stairs. Danny dashes up the stairs, but when we need to leave, he freezes at the top of the stairs and I have to pick him up and carry him down. What happened to his confidence?

A There are a number of reasons for dogs not wanting to tackle stairs, even enclosed ones. Danny's reluctance could be due to a medical condition, such as arthritis or hip dysplasia, so have that possibility checked out first. A key clue in this particular situation may be that outdoor stairs are often open, without solid risers between the steps. Danny is no dummy. To him, these stairs give him glimpses of the pavement far below, a vision as inviting as peering over the edge of a cliff.

Many dogs run easily up a flight of stairs but find the prospect of heading back down intimidating because they are less stable going down and more likely to slip or become unbalanced. Some dogs try to avoid stairs at all cost because of memories of a spill. Who wants to repeat that scary scenario?

It's tempting to give in to those pleading eyes and to offer him some soothing words and carry him down the stairs. But the problem with this is that it unintentionally fosters apprehension in your dog and can cause him to be even more fearful. Forget trying to scold Danny, too. Bullying him to go down the stairs solo without addressing his fear will only generate more behavior problems and weaken your relationship.

Instead, take it literally one step at a time with food rewards. Some of my favorite dog trainers recommend placing a mediocre treat (an ordinary dog biscuit) on the first step and then an irresistible treat (a piece of chicken breast or bacon) on the next step. Without saying a word or giving any nudges, let Danny scope out the situation with his nose and his eyes. Once he is brave enough to touch the stair with his paws, or even conquer one step to get the premium treat, heap on the praise as if he won an Oscar.

You won't be able to get Danny to be a stair champion, descending swiftly after one training session. Work a few minutes each day to expand his comfort level by placing the best treats on steps farther and farther down. During this transition when you are still toting him down the stairs, try whistling or singing a happy tune while striding confidently down the stairs. Danny may pick up on your cue that the stairs are not so scary after all.

SCAREDY-CAT DOGS

Noise-related phobias rank Number One among all sense-related phobias to our canine chums, according to Dr. Nicholas Dodman, director of the Animal Behavior Clinic at Tufts University. The author of several leading studies on phobias affecting companion animals, he lists several other fears that can escalate to phobias in dogs, including strangers, vacuum cleaners, and slippery floors.

Skidding to a Stop

Q We just replaced the carpet in our home with what we thought would be more pet-friendly flooring of tile and laminate. These smooth surfaces are much easier to keep clean and clear of pet hair, but Kelsey, our golden retriever, took a spill while turning a corner too fast during an indoor game of chasing a tennis ball with our teenage son. Now she is afraid of the footing and walks gingerly around the house. How can we restore Kelsey's confidence so she doesn't slink around the house?

A Your floors are pet friendly in that the materials make it easy to clean up puddles or other accidents, but they lack the traction that dogs need to move confidently around the house. Barring any physical injury, the spill probably made Kelsey feel a bit like Bambi on ice with legs splaying in all directions. To help her feel steady on her feet again, I recommend no more indoor chasing games with your son for a while!

Instead, guide her around the house on a long leash and encourage her to move slowly in different rooms and in different directions by luring her with great treats, like pieces of chicken. The idea is to rebuild her confidence and reassure her that she doesn't have to creep around like a snail. Strategically placed rugs with nonskid backing around doorways, in hallways, and in the center of larger rooms will give Kelsey more confidence when navigating.

It's also important to give Kelsey a suitable outlet to unleash her need for speed. Make sure she is getting enough exercise so that she doesn't have excess energy to burn inside. Convert casual strolls around the block into walks that cover more ground at a faster pace. Play fetch with her or treat her to playtime at a doggy day care or dog park. When she comes back home, she will be a tired and happy dog who is less apt to want to dash around indoors.

Finally, reinforce the *sit, stay,* and *lie down* cues so that during times you need to wash floors, or when a spill occurs, you can adequately control Kelsey's movement while you thoroughly dry your floor.

Telephone Terrorist

Q My Jack Russell terrier, Dexter, pesters me whenever I am trying to have a phone conversation. He barks, yips, tries to jump in my lap, and brings toys for me to toss. I used to think it was cute, but now I find it irritating. Why won't he leave me alone?

A Put yourself in your dog's place for a moment. As far as he can see, there is no one else in the room, but you're vocalizing. Naturally, he thinks you're talking to him. But when he responds, you ignore him, so he persists in trying to get your attention. If you do respond, in an effort to make him settle down, you are actually rewarding his irritating behavior. Unchecked attention-seeking behaviors can develop into serious behavior problems. Forcing you to pay attention to him gives your dog the wrong idea about who is the real leader in the house.

Since you used to regard this as cute, I imagine that you unintentionally encouraged this habit when Dexter was a wee pup. Now that he is bigger and bolder, his adorable act has become awfully annoying. It's time for a telephone intervention. If you can, use a phone in a room with a door and shut him outside while you're talking, even if it means telling your caller to wait a moment while you switch phones. Keep a chew toy or long-lasting treat within reach and toss it to him as you enter the room to talk on the phone.

Another option is to teach him that when the phone rings, he is to go to his crate, where he'll get a treat. You can start by putting him there before you dial a phone call so that he gets used to the idea of leaving you alone while you talk. Then practice by calling your home number with your cell phone and letting it ring a few times while you first reward him for sitting calmly, and then for staying, and then for going to his crate. As with all training, you will need to move in small steps to accomplish your goal.

Perhaps the most effective technique in the long run is to extinguish the behavior by completely ignoring Dexter when you are on the phone. In the beginning, practice by talking into your phone without dialing. Remain standing to keep him from jumping up or depositing toys in your lap. Turn your back on him and *do not* look at him or speak to him. Be prepared for his annoying behavior to increase at first, as he will work harder to get your attention. It takes time for the cold-shoulder routine to work and for your dog to start realizing that his actions don't generate *any* attention from you, good or bad. When he leaves you alone, and after you end your call, go over to him calmly and tell him *good settle,* and give him a treat for being a well-mannered dog. Jack Russells (now called

Parson Russells by the American Kennel Club), like most terriers, can be quite persistent and creative. Be glad he hasn't figured out a way to get his own cell phone!

Buried Treasures

Q Why does my dog seem so interested in burying his bones and even some of his favorite stuffed toys in the backyard? Even worse, he sometimes digs them up and brings the muddy mess back inside the house — always smiling and wagging his tail.

A Doggy doors have their benefits and their downsides. Some of my friends have the same complaint about their dogs. No one likes to come home and find muddy paw prints and smears from unburied canine treasures all over the floors.

Thousands of years ago, dogs did not know where their next meal would come from, so after a kill they would bury any uneaten food to hide it from scavengers. When they were hungry again, they would return to their cache and dig up their leftovers. The dirt also helped keep their food fresher longer by protecting it from sunlight. Your dog is just following that ancestral urge. Even though you feed your dog every day, you can't take that "must stash food for a hungry day" mentality out of him. The same goes for those extra toys he stashes away. Be glad he doesn't take other household items like the TV remote or your wallet — both have been known to disappear!

Keep in mind that dogs tend to bury extras, not essentials. Patrol your house and pick up any spare dog bones or toys. Limit his access to one bone and one toy at a time. Vary the type of dog bones and toys from time to time to keep him interested. By limiting the quantity and providing variety, you may lessen his motivation to take his treasures out to the backyard. Make his favorite digging spots less attractive by covering them with chicken wire or bricks or other objects that are not paw-friendly. And try offering your dog a less-destructive indoor option: Show him how he can bury his favorite bone or toy under a blanket instead.

Must-See TV

Q Growing up, I loved to watch *Lassie*, but my childhood dogs never seemed to pay attention to the television set. Now I enjoy programs on my wide, flat-screen TV and am interested to note that my dog seems to pay close attention to what's happening on the screen. He even barks when he hears a doorbell ringing on the TV and races to my front door. Why do some dogs seem to watch TV and others ignore it? What attracts them, the sight or the sound or both?

A Although some TV shows these days have gone to the dogs in terms of quality, it's not the programming that draws canine attention. Dogs do not see televised images as clearly as we do, but they certainly pick up the sounds. One reason for the difference between your childhood dog and your current companion might be that television sets during the *Lassie* days were far less clear and crisp than the vivid images and true-to-life sounds being delivered to flat-screen TVs of the digital age.

Even with modern technology, however, some dogs completely ignore the sights and sounds of all television programs. Others perk up when they hear a doorbell ring or a dog bark or a fire engine sound on TV. Some dogs seem to have a favorite movie that they will sit and watch intently. Others may paw at the moving images on the screen. One dog I know goes crazy when any kind of animal appears —

she tries to jump into the TV and has to be removed from the room! Other dogs just aren't interested or may even realize that the sounds aren't worth making a fuss over.

If you have a canine TV watcher, consider putting in a dog-themed movie or invite him to join you when you watch dog shows or agility events. You can even buy video or DVD programs specifically designed to interest dogs. Some people leave their television sets on when they leave their dogs home alone to provide some familiar background noise.

Getting over the Hump

Q Rocky, my boxer, is neutered, but that doesn't seem to matter to him. When visitors come over, Rocky runs up to greet and sniff and then tries to hump their legs. I am so embarrassed. Why does he do this, and how can I break him of this bad habit?

A Although intact male dogs are the most frequent offenders, neutered males and even spayed females are capable of humping legs and other objects. While it is usually viewed as a sexual action, some dogs mount as a form of play or when overexcited and unsure of the correct behavior. In your case, humping may be the way Rocky is alerting new guests that he is a powerful pooch. In neutered males and spayed females, humping signifies a bit of dominance and daring to push the boundaries. Your dog is challenging you and others to see how far he can assert himself with humans. It is vital to stop this habit before it escalates to more aggressive types of behavior. If your dog gets away with humping, he may begin growling and air-snapping at guests.

The peak time for this behavior to surface is during the challenging teen years, which for dogs fall between six months and two years, depending on the specific breed. The smaller the dog, in general, the faster the maturation. In Rocky's case, his physical strength and size might be spurring him on to continue humping since he can get away with it. He needs to learn that you are the leader of his pack and that guests also outrank him.

Breaking your dog of this habit will take time and patience. Start by making Rocky work for his needs and desires so that he understands that he has been demoted. He must sit to greet people, lie down and wait before receiving his food bowl, and wait at doorways for people to go through before him. (See Paying the Price, page 156.) To show Rocky what is acceptable behavior, put him on a leash when he is greeting people and tell him to sit and wait for them to come to him. Step on the leash and sharply tell him *stop* when he starts showing too much interest in their legs. If his behavior persists, discuss with your vet the possibility of temporarily using an antianxiety medication as an adjunct measure to let some air out of his Big Dog ego and to chill his libido.

You don't mention whether Rocky acts this way with other dogs, but I see humping at dog parks far too often. Size doesn't seem to matter, and sometimes the humping dog is smaller than the object of his mounting. A dog may mount another dog because he is confused about how to act when first meeting new dogs. Mounting is also an assertive way to show who ranks as top dog, literally. The "humper's" victory over the "humpee" is a way that dogs in the wild determine without fighting who earns the right to procreate with the best available bitches in the pack.

You can't always stop another person's dog from humping your dog, but you can teach your dog some defensive postures that may curb the mount-minded canine. If possible, get your dog to *sit*. A sitting dog is not as easy to hump as a standing one. You can also call your dog over to you. If possible, use your body to block access to your dog. Try to distract the other dog by tossing a tennis ball in the opposite direction.

A Tail's Tale

Q Often when my dog wakes up from a nap, he will start circling around to chase and try to catch his tail. He seems very determined to catch his tail. He spins around and around and seems almost frantic. I found it amusing at first, but now, it's a little disconcerting. What's the reason he does this?

A Researchers do not know why dogs chase their tails, but offer the theory that as predators, dogs instinctively react to movement. The blurry movement of a tail may be mistaken for a squirrel or rabbit and then the chase is on — in circles. Even tail-less dogs will romp around in circles on occasion. As long as the circling is done infrequently and stops within a few seconds, chalk it up to one of those weird but harmless canine behaviors.

For the occasional tail chaser, the answer may be as simple as a way to break up the monotony of a ho-hum afternoon. In mild forms, it can be the canine equivalent of people who twirl their hair, tap their feet, or smack their chewing gum. Some dogs seem to chase their tails to unleash bottled-up energy after being cooped up in a crate for a few hours or,

like your dog, after a long nap. Tail chasing offers a quick, easy way to get their muscles moving and their blood flowing. Some dogs discover that tail chasing rewards them by attracting attention. If you react by laughing, applauding, or offering treats, your dog quickly learns this is a good way to catch your eye and increase the handouts.

Some dogs, however, become tail-chasing addicts out of feelings of anxiety in stressful situations or because of a compulsive condition that requires professional help — and medication — from your veterinarian. If your dog's behavior persists for more than a moment after a nap, or you notice him grabbing at his tail, distract him with a favorite toy or treat. Give him a more acceptable behavior to perform like fetching a ball or Frisbee or joining you on a long, brisk walk in a place with lots of great scents to sniff.

Without intervention, a chronic tailchaser risks injury. Some dogs actually catch their tails and can hurt themselves by pulling and biting them. In extreme cases, these dogs may not stop even for food or to play with another dog. They literally spin so much that they collapse in sheer exhaustion on the floor. Bull terriers and German shepherds seem to be more genetically predisposed to tail chasing. (See Rhett Overcomes Anxiety, page 120, for more.)

Please do not encourage your dog to chase his tail or to follow the motions of a laser penlight or moving shadow. Either can become an obsessive or compulsive action.

Pass the Plastic, Please

Q Snickers, my yellow Labrador retriever, loves chewing on her plastic food bowl and anything within reach in our house that is made from plastic, such as soda bottles and storage bins. She is about nine months old. I'm worried that she will swallow bits of plastic and choke. I would also like to stop the destruction of household items. Why does she do this and how can I stop her?

A When it comes to Labrador retrievers, my veterinarian friend, Marty Becker, sums it up best by saying: "Labs chew 'til they're two and shed 'til they're dead." By this age, your puppy should be finished teething, but she is a natural-born chewer who needs a way to work her jaws. Snickers cannot distinguish a dog chew toy from the TV remote. She is on a constant quest to find something, anything, to chew.

First of all, any household with a puppy needs to be thoroughly puppy proofed so that tempting objects are out of sight and reach, and access is restricted to certain rooms. Young dogs, especially breeds like Labs, will occasionally nibble on shoes or try a taste test on the corner of your end table. It's part of the normal growing

up and exploring the environment stage. Snickers needs a suitable focus for her oral fixation such as beef- or chicken-flavored chew bones or hollow toys made of very durable, dog-resistant rubber that can be stuffed with treats. Both come in an array of sizes, shapes, and textures. Make sure you provide her with items that are specifically meant for chewing, rather than playing.

Snickers sounds like a good candidate for crate training, so you can control her environment when you can't actively supervise her. Regular exercise every day should also help curb her urge for inedible items. A quick and easy solution is to replace her plastic food and water bowls with others made of ceramic or stainless steel. These materials are easy to clean but hard to chew and won't retain the scent of food the way plastic does.

Spray Bitter Apple or sprinkle cayenne pepper on the objects of Snicker's attention, if they can't be put out of her reach. If she does pick up an inappropriate object in her mouth, startle her by clapping your hands or making a loud noise and saying *leave it!* Reinforce the *leave it* command by immediately presenting her with a more suitable object to mouth and heaping on the praise. The idea is to stop her from chewing on the wrong items by rewarding her for chewing the right items.

Please do not resort to scolding or grabbing her by the scruff of the neck. These forms of punishments won't help her understand what you want, but may cause her to become anxious and lose trust in you.

PICK A PICA PROBLEM

Dogs who constantly seek out plastic and other nonedible materials may be suffering from a condition known as pica. This is usually a psychological rather than a nutritional problem and can result in dogs eating gravel, rubber bands, wool socks, wooden baseboards, and even metal. Not only can these dogs damage their teeth — they can also suffer intestinal blockages that require surgery. If your dog regularly eats items that are not part of a normal canine diet, consult your veterinarian for possible solutions. This is definitely a problem that needs attention.

Bedtime Routine

Q Usually when she settles down for a nap, Maizie, my 11-year-old mixed breed dog, does the classic "turn around a few times before lying down" move. But sometimes she starts digging at the sofa and won't stop until she has made a big mess out of the slipcover. Once in a while, she will rumple up the runner in the hallway and then leave it there and go sleep somewhere else.

Sometimes she digs and bites at her bed so much that it gets all lumpy and then she doesn't want to lie on it! It often seems like she is more interested in trampling and digging than snoozing. Why does she do this?

A Your furniture-remodeling canine is tapping her ancient canine heritage when she circles, digs, and tramples. Well before the invention of sofas, blankets, and hallway runners, dogs in the wild had to sleep in the open if they weren't near a den. At bedtime, Maizie's ancestors huddled together for warmth and protection. Circling provided room for all to stake out a territory while remaining close. To protect themselves, they dug into the ground and trampled down the grass and other vegetation to make a nest far bigger than they needed. The reason? They wanted to project the idea that they were bigger than their actual size as a way to fool possible predators. If these nesting areas appeared large, the predator might decide to go elsewhere and hunt for a smaller, more vulnerable target.

Since she doesn't need to make a safe nest, Maizie's pawing and digging at blankets on the floor or rumpling the hallway runner are probably just her ways of making those items more comfortable for napping, just as many humans fuss with their pillows and blankets to make them feel just right before they sleep. After all her efforts to flatten them out or fluff them up, she may decide that they just won't work out as a makeshift bed, so she leaves the scene in search of a more suitable spot for snoozing.

PART IV

Unleashing a Dash of Doggy Discipline

Puppies and dogs don't enter our lives with owner's manuals that explain how to understand their quirks and avoid undesirable behaviors. In many cases, new owners think their new dog should behave just "because he loves me." Often, unfortunately, part of the reason behind our constant litany of *No! Bad dog! Drop it! Down! Bad, bad dog!* is poor pet parenting on our part. After all, dogs take their cues from what we say, how we say it, and what we do. They are not trying to misbehave; they just need to know what the rules are and how they fit in the family. It is our job to explain those things to them and to teach them how to become part of our lives.

This section addresses some of the most common challenges I've heard from frustrated owners. Take heart; you're in good company. Even professional dog trainers and animal behaviorists have their share of trying times. But with consistency, persistence, and kindness, you can convert a canine who is driving you crazy into a dog who is a sheer delight.

Puppy-Class Clown

Q My new puppy and I just enrolled in a puppy obedience class, but we're not exactly wowing the trainer or winning over classmates. Happy, aptly named, gets so excited in class that I sometimes lose grip of her leash and she is off playing with another puppy, trying to steal treats, and jumping in people's laps. I think we're going to flunk the class. Any advice on how I can gain control of this bundle of energy?

A First, kudos for enrolling Happy in a puppy class. It is essential for all pups and newly adopted adult dogs to become students in a reward-based obedience class. These classes do more than just teach your dog to come, sit, and stay. They provide an ideal venue for you to bond with your dog, to expose your pup to other dogs and people, and to learn the rules of canine etiquette. Some dogs are visual learners — puppy see, puppy do — so watching appropriate behaviors being rewarded may be good incentive. Having to go to class is usually good incentive for the owner to practice between sessions.

Don't worry; you and Happy will not become puppy-school dropouts. Remember that, as with all youngsters, a lot is going on both mentally and physically inside your personality-plus pooch. She is easily distracted and has no impulse control, so your job is to provide the limits for her behavior until she begins to understand what her role is.

Here are some insider secrets to achieving puppy-school success (and a diploma).

◆ **TAKE YOUR PUPPY FOR A WALK** lasting 20 to 30 minutes before arriving at your class. That way, she will have unleashed some of her pent-up energy and excitement.

◆ **ARRIVE FIVE TO TEN MINUTES EARLY** to allow your puppy to satisfy her uncontrollable need to meet and greet other classmates (both people and other puppies) and to relieve herself one last time. Many puppy classes have socializing as part of the lesson plan. For those that do not, this "play preview" can help Happy work through her excitement.

◆ **DON'T FEED HER BEFORE CLASS.** Depending on the time of the class, wait to serve up dinner until after the class or feed her only a half-portion, saving the rest for later. Hungry puppies are more motivated to perform for treats in class and won't need to take an urgent bathroom break.

◆ **KEEP YOUR HANDS FREE** by stashing your belongings in the trunk and clipping your car keys to your belt or tucking them in a pocket. You need your hands free to handle the leash, dole out treats, and give clear hand signals to your puppy.

◆ **WEAR CASUAL, COMFORTABLE CLOTHING.** If you wear shorts, expect to depart sporting grass-stained or muddy knees, not to mention scrapes and scratches from exuberant puppies. Stick with sneakers or other low-heeled, comfortable shoes with nonskid soles.

◆ **DON'T WEAR SUNGLASSES.** If the class is during the day, wear a visor or baseball hat to block out the sun. Your puppy needs to see your eyes at all times to grasp your messages.

◆ **HAND OUT ITTY-BITTY PORTIONS** of a highly palatable treat. You want to give your puppy a taste of a reward, just enough to swallow in few seconds. At first, give treats for every mini-success, because puppies tend to have the attention span of a gnat. Don't wait until your puppy completes all tasks before rewarding with a tiny treat.

◆ **BE BRAVE** and ask what you may think is a dumb question. What you perceive to be a strange behavior in your puppy — such as shredding toilet paper or splashing in her water dish — may be shared by someone else in your class who is too shy to ask.

◆ **KEEP YOUR PUPPY ON A LEASH** unless otherwise instructed by your trainer and give yourself enough space so your nosy puppy can't reach other classmates.

◆ Tap into vocal tones to help deliver your messages. Bring both your upbeat, happy, *good pup* voice and your stern, low, *knock it off* tone to class.

SCHOOL DAYS FOR YOUR DOG

A variety of schools exist to expand your dog's education. Classes run the gamut from puppy socialization to basic obedience to specialized sessions for dogs with testy temperaments. There are classes that teach dogs to become therapy canines and bring cheer to hospital patients and nursing home residents and classes that teach doggy etiquette, like Canine Good Citizenship.

The key is to look for professional dog trainers who rely on positive training techniques — not the use of physical punishment, chokers, or prong collars. I recommend that you contact the Association of Professional Dog Trainers to help you find the right trainer for you and your dog. You can learn more by visiting their Web site at www.apdt.com.

To Err Is Human

Q I feel like a terrible dog owner. Abby, my young retriever mix, doesn't always listen to me. She is really a sweet girl, but sometimes she becomes unruly. She chases our cat, jumps up on visitors, destroys the flowers in my garden, and tries to steal food from the counter. Sometimes I get frustrated and yell at her, even though I hate to do it. She cowers and leaves the room, and I feel awful and guilty. I am tired of saying no, no, no all the time. Help!

A Don't be too rough on yourself. Not even the most esteemed professional dog trainers are perfect each and every time they work with a dog. Mistakes happen. It's part of being human. One issue in your case is that Abby, like many large breeds, will take a little longer to mature than a smaller dog. Goldens and Labradors are generally considered "grown up" by age two or three, compared with Yorkshire terriers who have formed their adult brains by age one.

The key to successful training is to encourage your young dog to perform desired actions and to reward her when she nails a given command or task, rather than punishing her for bad behavior. It's also critical to provide suitable outlets for her to unleash her need to leap and chew. Over the years, I've identified several ways to avoid common training mistakes.

First, take on the role of leader, not bully. There is no need to raise your voice or berate your dog. Make sure the tenor of your voice is friendly, engaging, and confident. If you are feeling frustrated or impatient during the training lesson, Abby will pick up those anxious emotions and the lesson will be a failure. If you can be an effective teacher who relies on positive reinforcement techniques, however, you will earn her respect, instill her with confidence, and win her love and loyalty.

Second, puppies and young adult dogs are easily distracted. The only way to make your dog comply with your training is if you have her undivided attention. When you begin any training session, pick a place and a time where distractions are kept to a minimum. Start by calling your puppy by name and rewarding her for any eye contact with you. Once you are certain your pup knows her name, you can teach her *watch me* to sustain longer eye contact. Take a small food treat in your fingers and slowly bring it up to your face as you say *watch me*. Deliver the treat when she looks at you for at least two seconds. As she learns that she is rewarded for paying attention to you, she will be more motivated to look to you and await your next cue.

Third, you must be consistent, consistent, consistent. Decide which verbal and physical cues you want to use for *sit, lie down, stay,* and *come*. Then stick with them. If you use the word *stay* in one training session and the phrase *don't move* in the next, you create confusion. Be consistent with your commands and your dog will eventually catch on.

Fourth, opt for short training sessions. Unless you have an extremely attentive dog, training segments of 10 minutes or less will be the most effective. These mini-training sessions will work better for you, too, since they fit easily into your busy schedule. It's usually possible to squeeze in a short training lesson before you head off to work or when you get home after a long day.

Fifth, think Las Vegas! Gamblers are attracted to slot machines on the chance of hitting a jackpot. The machines, by design, do not deliver a payoff with each grab of the handle. Psychologists call this intermittent reinforcement. Apply this theory to training your dog. Once you've taught the basics, bolster compliance by offering a treat intermittently. Keep Abby guessing about when she'll be rewarded, and she'll work harder for that tasty jackpot. You can bet on it!

Finally, take your training routine on the road. Abby may become a picture of perfect obedience inside your living room but act like a canine Dennis the Menace at the dog park. She needs to learn that she must obey you, no matter where she is and how many distractions surround her. Once you have success in the confines of your home, gradually reinforce these commands with her in other settings. You need to start with small steps and build up to success.

PAYING THE PRICE

In my view, the Nothing in Life Is Free (NILIF) program offers the best payoff for most dogs and their owners. With NILIF, your dog complies with your commands and you do not need to bully or use physical force.

The idea is that you bolster your leadership and cultivate your dog's respect for you by controlling all his resources. Specifically, you determine when you put his food bowl down and when you pick it up, rather than responding to his begging or letting him guard his bowl. You set the time for playing with toys and when game time ends. You initiate grooming and petting sessions.

By controlling his resources, you elevate your status in the eyes of your dog. I particularly like this positive method of training because it works on a wide range of canine personalities, including shy, easily distracted, high energy, and pushy dogs. Shy dogs gain confidence; distracted dogs develop focus and patience; pushy dogs learn canine manners.

Here's how NILIF works. Start by giving your dog the cold shoulder when he demands your attention. Ignore him if he paws your hand, barks at you, or brings a toy to get you to pet or play with him. Don't utter a single syllable or push him away. Just act as if he is invisible. This is not meant to be rude or cruel. Rather, you are training your dog to understand that he cannot demand your attention any time he desires. The light bulb will turn on in his brain as he realizes that it is you, not he, who calls the shots in the household.

NOTE: Be prepared for an increase in unwanted behavior as you implement your new strategy. Your dog will try harder at first, since his tactics worked in the past. Do not give in!

All members of the family must participate in the new house rules. Let them know that from now on, your dog must earn his paycheck (praise, treats, playtime) with proper behavior. At mealtime, ask your dog to *sit* and *wait* before you put the bowl down. When you want to play one of his favorite games, such as fetching a tennis ball, tell him to *lie down* before you toss the ball again. When you are done with the game, tell him *game over,* pick up the ball, and put it out of his reach. Do this calmly and walk away. The key to success is being consistent. Every time you want to toss your dog a small treat, have him do something — sit or do a trick — before you hand over the tasty morsel. When you approach the front door to walk him, make sure he knows that you always exit and enter doors before him. At your dog training class, your dog must do what you've asked before he gets a treat.

The bottom line is that NILIF establishes a clear ranking in the household with you in the number one spot. It is done without meanness but rather as a simple fact of life. NIFIL is the canine version of saying *please.* In time, your dog will come to view you as the Provider of All Things Wonderful and you will be amazed at how much he will come to appreciate this clarity and be more responsive to your cues.

Hey! Come Back Here!

Q I thought teaching my dog to come to me would be a snap. Boy, was I wrong! Higgins is a six-month-old mixed breed with a mind of his own. I find myself having to yell at him to come back to me and scolding him when he finally does. It's getting worse. When I take him to the local dog park, I have to chase him to put the leash on him when it is time to go. How can I get Higgins to come when I call him?

A There are three basic commands that are doggone vital: *come, sit,* and *stay.* These commands can be lifesavers. An obedient dog responds to *come* and turns toward you rather than chasing a cat into a busy street. Unlike a trained dog who ignores his owner's calls in favor of an alluring odor, it sounds as though Higgins has never learned to come in the first place. When he is running around loose, he probably has no idea what you want and no real interest in finding out. Higgins is a canine teenager and has entered the stage in life when he feels the need to test and challenge authority. He needs to know clearly who's in charge, and that should be you.

When you overuse the word *come,* it becomes meaningless. Repetition of a cue that is being ignored just teaches the dog that he doesn't have to do anything. Some dogs wait until their owners say *come* for the 12th time before they stop running and turn their heads. Others decide that *come* actually means *keep running around sniffing until my owner grabs me.*

Another easy misstep is to over-speak when you want Higgins to come. You must pick a cue and use it consistently. If you call out, "Hey Higgins, I want you to come here right now, I'm not joking, Higgins, I really mean it, I want you to come now," Higgins, in true doggy fashion, is most likely to translate all that chatter into "Higgins, blah, blah, blah, blah" and will never respond to your call. It got lost in translation.

There are many ways to teach Higgins to come when you call, but here are three of my favorites. Conduct your training sessions in a confined area like your backyard or a hallway or any place without a lot of distractions or places to escape. You want him to focus on you. (See Have Nose, Must Travel, page 35, for another good method.)

Game Plan A: Change your attitude. You mentioned that you scold Higgins when he finally does return. It is easy to be a bit peeved when your dog dashes off. But because of your harsh tones, Higgins associates the word *come* with reprimands. Why should he return only to be scolded? Try switching to a new word to get your dog to come back. Instead, say *here* or *now* or even *bye.* I used the latter on my former dog, Jazz, when he stopped heeding the *come* cue. I would simply say *bye,* turn my back on him, and walk in the opposite direction. He was back in a flash by my side. Even when Higgins seems to take his sweet time at returning, never yell at him for coming back.

Game Plan B: Make it child's play by modifying the hide-and-seek game. In your house, have a family member or friend keep Higgins on a leash as you scurry into another room out of his view. Your helper then unleashes Higgins as you call out *Higgins, come!* in an upbeat, happy voice. As soon as he finds you, give him a treat, say *yes!* and repeat the game in a different room. This makes finding you lots of fun for Higgins.

Game Plan C: Play tag. Lightly tap Higgins on the back and say, "Tag, you're it!" Then race away. When Higgins pursues you and reaches you, praise him and give a treat. If he doesn't follow you, stop a few feet away, keep your back to him, and bend down. Pretend you are looking at the world's most fascinating blade of grass or carpet fiber. Curiosity will get the best of Higgins, and he will come up to investigate what is so darn riveting. Again, praise and treat. The goal is to always have your dog chase after you, not the other way around.

Practice all three of these games in your home and in confined areas without a lot of distractions. Please do not let him run loose in open places near streets where he could get hit by a car. Always end these mini-sessions on a good note. When he comes back quickly, praise and treat and move on. Once Higgins consistently heeds your calls to him, then test his responsiveness in a backyard or dog park with only one or two other dogs around. Gradually, build up his recall until Higgins responds even in high canine traffic, like at a dog park on a Saturday morning.

Off the Sofa!

Q My three-year-old beagle is a delight, but he has one vice: He insists on jumping up onto my furniture. His spiky hair gets embedded in the upholstery until it's nearly impossible to clean. I've tried putting old bed sheets on the furniture when I'm gone, but when I come home I find the sheets on the floor and Peppy happily snoozing on the sofa. I got him about a year ago from a rescue group and can only assume that he was allowed to get up on the sofa in his previous home. I'm planning to purchase nicer furniture and upgrade the interior of my house soon. Before I do, I want to find a way to end Peppy's possession of my sofa. How can I accomplish this?

A Credit Peppy for having the good sense to bypass boring bare floors and seek a comfy sofa for his snooze sessions. However, it's your house and he needs to play by your rules. First, you need to provide him with a designated spot of his own. Before you begin picking out your new furniture, buy Peppy a comfy bed and put it in a spot where he will still feel like part of the family. When you are home, have him lie on it and reward him for spending time there. The world of canine décor has exploded recently, and you have many choices of functional but fashionable doggy beds and other canine comforts (even a small sofa of his own, if you like!) that will blend with your style of furnishing, be it rustic or elegant or anything in between.

As you begin your mission to relocate Peppy from the sofa to his own furniture, you need to make your furniture uninviting. Use fitted bed sheets instead of flat sheets so that you can tuck them in snugly. When you leave the house, pile items on your furniture to make naptime anything but pleasant. Take a plastic carpet runner, turn it upside down so that the hard points are facing upward, and lay it across your sofa and recliner. Or put heavy boxes of books on the furniture before you leave the house so there is no space for even a determined beagle.

> **SNIFF IT OUT!**
> Some of the doggiest addresses in North America include Bark River, Michigan; Bassett, California; Yorkshire, New York; and the Canadian provinces of Labrador and Newfoundland.

Sitting Pretty

Q I just adopted my first puppy. What's the best way to teach Clara to sit when I ask her? I don't like having to force her into position by pushing down on her rump. She does sit when I do that, but only for a couple of seconds before bouncing right back up to lick my face. She's adorable and small now, but will probably be 80 pounds when she grows up, so I know it's important to teach her while I can still physically handle her.

A I consider *sit* to be one of the essential cues to be learned by all dogs, and you are right to want to teach your pup while she is still small. *Sit* is your first choice when you want to keep your puppy from doing something you don't like, such as chasing a fly in the house or happily tackling a visitor at the door. When in doubt, have your dog sit. It stops her undesired action and shifts her attention to you. Also, a dog who sits politely is a pleasure to be around and always wows onlookers in public.

There are two "hands-off" ways to teach your pup to sit. The first is all about timing. Whenever your puppy flops into a sit position on her own, say *Sit! Yes!* and give her a treat if you can or tell her what a smart girl she is. Try to do this every time you see her sit. During this training time, keep a treat bag on your belt loop or stash a few treats in your pocket so you can immediately reward the desired behavior. Some smart pups quickly learn to rush up to their owners and sit because they have been conditioned to receive treats. Remember, however, to make sure she is still sitting when you hand over the treat.

The second method taps into the power of gravity to get your pup to sit nicely. Place a small treat in one hand. Slowly glide your other hand up and over your dog's head while she is standing. In a positive tone, say *Clara, sit*. As you guide your hand up and over your dog's head, she will arch her head back to follow. The instant her rump hits the floor, tell her *Sit! Yes!* and hand over the treat. Repeat these steps four or five times per session. In time, your pup should sit whenever you say that magic word or convey it by using that over-her-back hand signal.

Training your puppy that great things happen when she complies and sits nicely will help you in your training sessions for other cues as well. Practice having her sit often and reward her with treats and praise. Once she understands the cue, you can give treats intermittently to reinforce the notion that desired behaviors reap rewards. A dog who sits at the curb attached to a loose leash while waiting for the light to change often earns compliments about her good behavior from onlookers. Dogs, just like us, love positive attention and these comments will help motivate her to sit on cue.

Hey, Hey, Why Don't You Stay?

Q My neighbor Paul has a very obedient Rottweiler named Gus. If Paul tells him to stay, Gus will sit or lie down and not move until Paul tells him it's okay. He waits quietly while Paul picks up milk at the corner store or has a cup of coffee in a café. My big friendly mutt Moose won't stay put for a second. Maybe I have a little bit of canine envy. How can I get Moose to behave the way Gus does?

A Sometimes we need our dogs to remain in one place until we say they can move. Teaching your dog to *stay* is handy when you want him not to bolt out of your house or car when you open the door or give chase when the family cat enters the room. And, as with Gus, it's nice to have a dog who will wait quietly while you do an errand. You want Moose to realize that if he stays in one spot until you say otherwise, he will be safe. He learns that even if you disappear from view into a store, you will always return (with praise for his good behavior, of course!) for him.

You can teach Moose to stay on cue, but don't expect overnight success. First of all, he should know *sit* and *down* before beginning on this more complicated behavior. As you teach Moose to *stay*, keep the training sessions short and fun and always end on a good note. If Moose seems to struggle a bit, don't move forward until he consistently succeeds in the earlier steps.

Mastering the *stay* command involves duration, distance, and distractions. At first, expect Moose to stay for just a moment while you stand next to him and there is nothing else going on around you. Put him on a long leash so you can control him if he tries to move. Your goal is to gradually expand the length of time Moose complies and the distance between the two of you. The final element involves Moose staying put despite distractions like other dogs or squirrels.

In training a dog, you need eye contact and undivided attention from him. First, teach Moose the *watch me* cue by saying his name and telling him *watch me* as you take a small food treat and move it toward the side of your eye. The goal is to get him to watch the treat move. When he does, hand over the treat. This teaches him to focus on you.

> **BREED BYTE**
>
> **During the Middle Ages in Germany, butchers traveling to buy livestock would fasten their moneybags around the muscular necks of their Rottweilers to dissuade would-be thieves.**

Next, put him in a down or sit position. Wait a second or two before you say *stay!* as you use your hand in a motion like a traffic cop halting oncoming cars and then reward with a treat. Gradually delay the reward to teach your dog that he is to stay put. With each successful *stay,* slowly extend the time before you reward from two to five to ten seconds and on up to a minute. If Moose should get up and move before the designated time, do not give a treat. Do not punish him, either — just return him to his original position and tell him to *stay* again.

When you are ready to have Moose move, give him a specific release word and hand signal. I use the word *okay* with a sweeping motion of my open-palmed hand. You could say *we're done* or *release* — any term you will remember easily.

When Moose is consistantly solid for a minute, add the distance element by putting Moose in a *stay* and moving about five feet away while he is still on a leash. Reward him for staying until you return to him. Slowly build on his success by dropping the leash and expanding the distance between you. As he learns, add to the difficulty by walking behind him and moving around him. Again, if he breaks from his *stay*, just return him to position and start again.

The final step is to introduce distractions. After all, your dog does not live in a bubble. Things happen — a squirrel will suddenly appear on the sidewalk, or a skateboard will whiz by — and Moose may want to give chase. That's where the *stay* command keeps him by your side. Start with mild distractions, such as having someone clap his hands or wave his arms. Take your training outside and have a friend walk by as you tell Moose to *stay*. Ask your neighbor Paul to help for a few training sessions by walking Gus past while Moose shows how much he's learned. Go slowly and encourage Moose. Most of all, be patient. Deliver treats and praise only when your dog ignores the increasingly tempting distractions and stays put.

Ignoring Temptation

Q My elderly mother lives with us and needs to take medication for her heart and for high blood pressure. I worry that she may accidentally drop a pill on the floor and Pebbles, my pug, will think it's food, eat it, and get sick. Pebbles constantly has her nose to the ground, trying to sniff out anything edible. Is there any way I can teach her not to eat something she shouldn't?

A You are right to be concerned about Pebbles accidentally mistaking a pill for a food find. With her small size, she could become very sick and possibly even die from swallowing human medication. However, it is canine nature to explore using the nose and the mouth. After all, our thumbless dogs can't pick up a tempting

object in their paws and scrutinize it. They are designed to sniff and sample.

It is far better to be safe and prepared by teaching your dog to *leave it* and *drop it*. These behaviors work in partnership, so think of them as the Dynamic Duo for Dog Safety. They are effective whenever you need your dog to ignore something within reach or to release something already in her mouth, such as the TV remote or a bottle of pills.

To begin, put Pebbles on a leash and practice in a quiet room in your house to avoid other distractions. Teach her to *leave it* first. Your mission is to stop her before she can put the object in her mouth. Put a treat in your hand and make a fist. Without her knowing, hide a second treat nearby. Let Pebbles smell your hand. She will probably lick your hand, paw at it, and try to get you to surrender the treat to her. Practice some patience. Wait for her to give up and stop pawing at your closed hand for a few seconds. Then, praise her and hand over the hidden treat. Repeat this until Pebbles catches on that by honoring your *leave it* request, she gets the goodies.

Then you can up the ante. Put Pebbles on a leash and bring out two types of treats: so-so and delicious. Drop a piece or two of the so-so treat on the ground in front of Pebbles and tell her to *leave it*. Restrain her with the leash if necessary. Once she ignores the temptation, hand over a few of the better treats to her and praise her. Practice this often on your walks to reinforce the desired behavior in different situations.

Next, teach the *drop it* command. Start by enticing Pebbles with one of her B-list toys. Let her put the toy in her mouth and play with it for a minute or so and then show her one of her all-time favorite toys or a yummy treat. As soon as she opens her mouth, say *drop it*. You are pairing the phrase *drop it* with the behavior — releasing the toy from her mouth. Praise her when she lets go of the toy and approaches you to take the new treat. Vary the objects (always getting her to trade up to a more desirable object) to expand her understanding of the *drop it* request.

These phrases should be in every dog owner's repertoire. My neighbor Flo can testify to how valuable it is to master these commands. Buddy, her miniature schnauzer, likes to steal household objects and stash them in his bed. To him, it's a game. To Flo, it's a crime. One day, Flo accidentally left her hearing aid on the end table. Buddy quickly confiscated it and started to dash off. Instead of giving chase, Flo told Buddy to *drop it* in a calm tone. He did immediately and then sat. Her hearing aid was unharmed and Buddy got rewarded with a special food treat — not for stealing the hearing aid, but for obeying the *drop it* command.

A final pointer: resist shouting *drop it* in an urgent tone while you chase after your dog. If you are overly annoyed or emotional, your dog will either swallow the goody fast or run with it, thinking it has value. The best strategy is to speak calmly (even though you may be quite upset) and reward with a high-value treat.

POISON HOTLINE

If you ever suspect that your dog has swallowed human medication or any toxic substance, call the ASPCA Animal Poison Control Center Hotline toll-free at 1-888-426-4435. Their Web site is www.aspca.org. Please note there is a consultation fee that can be applied to your credit card, but it is worth the price if you save your pet's life. Put their number and the contact info of your own veterinarian and the nearest emergency veterinary clinic on a card and post it in a handy spot near the phone for quick reference.

Hand-Me-Down Crate

Q We are planning to get a second puppy to be a playmate for Gladys, our schnauzer-poodle mix. Gladys is nearly 18 months old and is finally being trusted in our home without being confined inside her crate when we're at work. We leave her crate door open and when she wants to take a nap, she heads into it. Soon we will be adopting Jake, a young golden retriever-poodle mix. How can we convert Gladys's crate for Jake without her getting upset or territorial?

A I'm a big fan of crate training. Dogs are den animals. They don't demand much. They don't clamor for a giant master bedroom or a pile of feather pillows, but they do want and need a quiet place in the house that they can call their own. Handing down Gladys's crate to the new pup may seem to make sense, but I encourage you to purchase a second crate for Jake. For one thing, unless her crate is quite large, it is likely that he will quickly outgrow it, as he will certainly be a bigger dog. More important, if Gladys likes her crate and uses it as her established den, you will avoid problems by letting her keep her spot and providing a separate cozy spot for Jake.

Furthermore, in case you need to evacuate your house in an emergency, your two dogs can be placed inside their individual crates for safe transportation and temporary housing. Crates used in cars allow your dogs to travel safely and keep them from getting injured in the event you must make a sharp turn or sudden stop.

That said, if you still don't want two crates, then here is how to ensure that Gladys is gracious about handing hers down to newcomer Jake. Before Jake arrives, treat Gladys to a new doggy bed. Make sure it is comfy and that you place it in the same area where the crate is now. She has established this area of your home as her turf. Have her lie on her bed and reward her for spending time there.

Next, thoroughly wash the crate with an antibacterial cleaning product and let it dry completely. Do not use products containing ammonia because they mimic urine odor. Before Jake's arrival, keep the crate out of Gladys's sight for a few days to diminish her memories of her former canine bedroom. Then move the crate to a different location in your house for the newcomer. Provide new bedding that does not have Gladys's scent. Young puppies are big chewers, so I would advise you to use clean, old towels for bedding and wait to get a proper bed until Jake stops chewing. I learned this the expensive way with a puppy who chewed up three foam-filled beds before I switched to towels.

As you begin to crate train Jake, curb any interference from Gladys by tossing her favorite toy or treat onto her new bed. Tell her to go get it, praise her when she does, and then have her *sit* or *stay* while you work with young Jake. Whenever Gladys goes to her bed, praise her. Make a big deal out of her fancy new bed. Make it seem like a million-dollar mansion in canine real estate terms.

Of course, it can be challenging for Gladys to sit nicely while you spend time crate-training Jake. So consider ushering her into another room or enclosed yard with a favorite chew toy. Or take her for a long walk beforehand so that she's tired and more likely to nap and not interfere with the training session. Also, remember to book special one-on-one time with Gladys. Treat her to a fun walk or play with her in the backyard occasionally when Jake is in his crate taking a puppy nap.

CRATE DOS AND DON'TS

Follow these guidelines to guarantee that your dog will regard his crate or portable kennel as a great place.

Select a crate only big enough for your puppy to stand up and turn around in easily. If you buy a crate to match your puppy's eventual adult size, temporarily insert a divider until he gets larger.

Let your puppy investigate inside the crate on his own. Encourage his curiosity by tossing a toy or a few treats inside.

Feed your puppy in his crate. Quietly close the door while he eats and then open the door after he eats and let him go outside to go to the bathroom.

Make the interior of the crate comfortable with a blanket or old bath towel and a chew toy to keep him occupied.

Never put your puppy in his crate as punishment. Select a different time-out location, like a bathroom, when you need to stop an unwanted behavior.

Do not keep your dog in a crate longer than four or five hours at a time.

Who's the Boss?

Q At first, we thought it was cute when our Scottish terrier puppy growled playfully at us whenever we tried to take a toy away from her or keep her from stealing a sock. But Mimi is now nearly a year old and her growls don't seem so harmless. She hasn't bitten anyone, but she definitely sounds like she means business. What can we do to keep this behavior from escalating?

A It may seem amusing when a puppy commandeers a sock or keeps you at bay when you try to take a toy from her, but this is a very bad habit. Left undisciplined, many dogs will begin to view themselves as the leader of the household and will progress from growling to snapping at, or even biting, people who challenge them.

This type of aggression may surface between 12 and 24 months of age as a dog gains physical and social maturity. If aggression directed at owners is allowed, the dog can become uneasy and anxious, and the owners frustrated and fearful, setting up a vicious cycle of behavior. Untreated, this canine bullying will only intensify. This is a particularly important time for you to be firm, fair, and consistent. Be aware that showering such a dog with affection, giving her unearned treats, and allowing her free reign of the house will reinforce this behavior, because the dog will feel that her top dog attitude is being rewarded.

In Mimi's case, you need to become a VIP (Very Influential Person) in her view while she is demoted to PHP (Pretty Humble Pup). Instead of trying to match growl for growl, you need to become the household's benevolent leader whom your dog looks up to, the person who has more influence over her than anyone or anything else in the world. (See Paying the Price on page 156.) Whenever Mimi shows any sign of aggression, calmly put her in a bathroom. Close the door and give her a brief time-out (less than five minutes). When you open the door, ignore her for about 30 seconds. Banishment and withdrawal of attention are the most potent forms of correction because they remove a dog's ability to control a situation.

You also need to work on properly training Mimi so that she understands basic obedience cues. (See Ignoring Temptation on page 169 for tips on teaching her to *drop it,* for example.)

Have everyone in your house and regular visitors practice these new rules. By becoming a better leader who is consistently gentle but firm, you will have better control of the sit-

BREED BYTE
Dalmatian puppies are born pure white. Their trademark black spots pop up as they mature. A few Dalmatians have liver-colored spots.

uation and Mimi will be likely to stop growling and display better behavior. If her behavior does not improve, however, I favor being pro-active and seeking help from an animal behaviorist before growls turn into lunges or biting attacks.

Having Spot Find His Spot

Q When I get ready to leave the house and when I first come in the front door, my dog is always underfoot. She wiggles her whole body, wags her tail a mile a minute, tries to jump on me, and gives me kisses. More than once, I've spilled a bag of groceries because I've tripped over her or tried to reach down to pet her in an attempt to quiet her down. I love Katie, but what can I do so that I can come and go without this over-the-top demonstration of affection?

A Now you know how a rock star or other celebrity feels when surrounded by adoring but obnoxious fans. Katie is doing all she can to deliver canine love your way, even at the sacrifice of some groceries. Her slightly pushy behavior has worked so far in getting what she wants, which is your attention. Here is one way you can redirect Katie's enthusiasm to allow you to walk in and out without having to play dodge dog. (See Clingy Canine, page 218, and Look Out! Launching Lab!, page 74, for other strategies.)

Situate a dog bed somewhere near your door where your dog can see but not be in the way. Whenever you have five minutes and are in a patient mood, call Katie. Have her *sit* and *stay* somewhere else in the room while you toss a treat on the doggy bed. Make her *stay* until you excitedly call out *Find your spot!* as you point to the treat on the bed.

Encourage Katie as she dashes to the bed to grab the treat. Praise her and have her *stay* on the bed for a few seconds.

Repeat this scenario several times. With each success, extend the time that she stays on her bed. Now, you're ready to toss a treat and ask her to find her spot and stay there as you head out the door. Give her premium treats when she remains on the bed when you enter the house. *Find your spot!* works wonders when you greet someone at your door, leave your dog behind to go shopping, or want your dog not to be underfoot.

In my house, *find your spot!* generates a lot of anticipation and excitement because Chipper never knows which of her favorite treats she will get until she lands on the doggy bed in the family room. Sometimes, I put peanut butter in a hollow synthetic bone. Other times, I give her a dental chew or a handful of dried turkey treats. We both know the routine. I grab the treats and my purse as Chipper waits on the stairway landing. Then, I call out in a happy tone *find your spot!* That's her cue to race down the stairs where she does a triumphant leap onto the bed and happily awaits her surprise goodies.

I keep a jar of treats in the garage so that before I even come in the door, I can say *find your spot!* and she will be waiting for me on her bed as I walk in. She knows to wait there until I toss her a treat. I use this command at bedtime, too, to get Chipper to tuck herself in her bed upstairs so I can brush my teeth and wash my face without tripping over her.

Love on a Leash

Q Callie, my happy Brittany spaniel, yanks and pulls constantly on the leash when I take her for a walk. If she wants to smell something a few feet ahead, she takes off with no regard for my shoulder or wrist. She charges back and forth in front of me or drags behind to check out different smells. Walking her is not fun. It's trying and tiring. I scold her but she just ignores me and keeps pulling. What can I do so that she walks politely on a leash?

A Sounds like walking Callie is literally a drag, but you have plenty of company. There are legions of leash-yanking dogs all over the globe. Right now, the problem is that Callie doesn't understand that you want her to behave a certain way on your walks. She is just excited to be outside smelling all those great scents. It can be challenging to reign in a dog on a "gotta sniff here, there, and everywhere" canine quest. Success hinges on improving her focus on you, using the right equipment, and developing your "benevolent boss" status, plus a lot of patience and practice.

What doesn't work is yanking back. When a dog feels pressure on her throat, she responds by leaning into that pressure to get away from it. Yanking on the leash doesn't teach her to stop pulling and can injure her neck and trachea. Because you are just continuing the cycle, you keep losing this leash tug-of-war, which reinforces her determination to yank even more.

You need to start by increasing your own "curb appeal" so that Callie pays attention to you rather than to that squirrel scampering up the oak tree, that stray soccer ball kicked in your path, or that beckoning smell left on your route by the cute Westie up the street. Before you head out the door, prepare a bag of treats cut into tiny pieces. Teach Callie the *watch me* command, so she will look your way when you speak those magic words. Practice inside the house for a few days first and then on the sidewalk in front of your house. Then walk a bit and call *watch me* again. Treat her sporadically so Callie never knows when a reward will occur. Dogs will perform more consistently if they aren't rewarded every single time they respond.

You also need the right tools. Please avoid choke or prong collars. Some dogs react to these by becoming testy and aggressive, and if used improperly, these collars can cause injury. Instead, opt for a nylon halter, which fits behind your dog's ears with a loop over the nose. The leash is attached to a metal ring below your dog's chin. It comes with directions, but if you're not sure how to properly fit one on your dog, seek the help of a dog trainer or your veterinarian.

The halter works by applying pressure to the dog's nose instead of her throat. Because the nose is more sensitive than the neck, she will back away from the pressure rather than leaning into it. You can also use a no-pull harness that puts pressure on the dog's chest. Remember that the halter and other similar types of equipment should be viewed as training aids, not instant solutions to the problem. It is not the equipment but how it is used that makes it effective or dangerous.

Let me emphasize that the halter is not a muzzle. It doesn't prevent your dog from being able to breathe, pant, drink, chew, or pick up toys or treats. It does control her head movement without causing pain and with a minimum of effort, which will save your shoulder muscles. It also doesn't need to be a lifelong accessory. Once your dog learns the habit of walking politely, you can gradually wean her off the head halter if you want to.

Introduce the new gear inside the house at first. Let Callie sniff and inspect it. Put it on her and distract her with treats if she tries to rub it off (something many dogs will

attempt). Keep the mood light and playful and do not reprimand her for trying to remove it. Then take her out for a short walk with the goal of teaching her to associate the head halter with two favorite doggy pleasures: going for a walk and getting treats.

As a dog's head goes, so goes the direction of her body. A slight tug on the leash will automatically move Callie's head back to look at you. No longer focused on moving forward, she should stop and look to you to see what's next. Let a few seconds pass, and then resume the walk or abruptly change directions or pace. Keep her guessing. Reward her for keeping her attention on you.

If *watch me* and the halter aren't working as well as you'd like, act like a tree. Trees don't move. If Callie starts to yank, stop and remain still. Do not move forward again until the leash is slack. Or take a couple quick steps backward until she pays attention. Once she is focused on you, resume walking and dole out treats only when the leash is slack, not tight. When Callie is walking easily, point out her good behavior by using the proper word. Some people say *heel,* but I prefer *walk nicely.* It sounds more civilized. Praise Callie and treat her for her stretches of walking nicely.

Training a dog to stop tugging on her leash takes time and patience, but the payoff is worth it. The two of you can enjoy your walks together, and your role as leader will become more firmly established with your dog, which will benefit your whole relationship.

Cosmo Cools It

COSMO, A FOUR-YEAR-OLD neutered cocker spaniel, behaved like a barroom bouncer when his owners Gaby and Tony asked him to do anything he didn't want to do. He gave clear warnings, increasing from growls to displaying his teeth to actually biting, when they tried to groom him or move him off their bed. Twice, Cosmo nipped Tony when he tried to put a choke chain on him. At night Cosmo took over their bed, reacting strongly if disturbed from a deep sleep and snapping while settling down.

Despite of his aggressive displays, Cosmo would some-times roll over and release a small amount of urine when he was excited or feeling submissive. This behavior is not uncommon among cocker spaniels. On the positive side, Cosmo was not aggressive around other dogs, while he ate, or when resting inside his crate. The couple could easily take his dish or toys away from him.

My diagnosis was that Cosmo suffered from moderate dominance aggression, social status aggression, anxiety, and submissive/excited urination. No medical condition was found, but his front right footpad never grew completely, which may explain why he was hypersensitive to having his nails trimmed. Instead of trying to clip all his nails at once, I advised Gaby and Tony to clip one nail at a time and reward him after each one with a high-value treat, to develop a positive association with grooming. I suggested that they immediately replace the choke collar they were using with a halter-type collar. In Cosmo's case, the use of the choker only fueled his aggression.

Addressing this dog's undesirable behavior took patience and time. Cosmo was placed on an antianxiety medication, which helped him become calmer, especially when awakening. The owners took some basic safety precautions, including not permitting him to sleep on their bed any longer. Instead of leaning over a sleeping Cosmo to wake him, I encouraged them to stand at a safe distance and call out Cosmo's name to wake him. The goal was to try as much as possible not to set Cosmo up for failure by trying to force him off a bed or startling him from a deep sleep.

Cosmo had never received any formal dog training, so we worked on teaching reliable compliance with basic behaviors: *sit, down, stay, come,* and *quiet.* If Cosmo displayed aggression, he was placed in a closed bathroom for a short duration. On a positive note, we tapped Cosmo's favorite activity, playing fetch, and had him earn playtime.

After just a month of behavior modification and medication, Cosmo's behavior improved. He stopped growling when being groomed or told to move. He listens to Gaby and Tony and appears to be a more contented cocker spaniel.

Contributed by Patrick Melese, DVM

Go-Go-Go Lab

Q Tasha, my black Labrador retriever, never seems to tire out. I can play fetch with her for over an hour and she still wants to play. I take her to a doggy day care three times a week, and the manager tells me that she romps all day with the other dogs. Yet when I come to pick her up, she has energy to burn. She is almost two years old. Will she ever tone down her activity level? I love her but wish there were times where she was quiet and calm.

A Some dogs do seem to behave like furry wind-up toys that never wind down. These overactive dogs do everything at top speed and rarely seem to nap or relax. When not playing, high-energy dogs may pace, yap non-stop, or display an unquenchable desire for attention. In

Tasha's case, her breed is well known for having plenty of energy and for maturing late, but even the most rollicking retriever should settle down sometimes. It is possible that her behavior is caused by an underlying health problem. Though rare, dogs can be diagnosed with hyperkinesis, the canine equivalent of attention-deficit hyperactivity disorder. Always in a hurry, and sometimes frantically active, dogs with this medical condition possess rapid heart rates and won't stop until they are completely exhausted. Book an appointment with your veterinarian to give Tasha a complete physical exam to rule out any medical causes and review any medication that she may be taking, because certain medications can trigger anxiety and hyperactivity as side effects.

If she is indeed just a high-energy gal, you can address some behavior remedies. You're on the right path by playing fetch with her and letting her use up her ya-ya's at doggy day care. In addition to burning up energy, try introducing some fast-paced, combination commands designed to work her brain *and* her body. For example, ask Tasha to perform doggy push-ups: a rapid series of *sit, down, sit, down*. Once Tasha gets the hang of it, she will look like she is actually performing a canine version of our push-up. These fast movements are fun for lively dogs.

Expand her trick repertoire and teach her to do three rollovers in a row or have her circle you three times before you hand out a treat. In addition to walks and day care, let Tasha swim and fetch balls in safe waters when the weather permits. Swimming doesn't tax the joints, provides a great aerobic workout, and is a natural activity for Labs. Check out Canine Jocks Rule on page 200 for more ideas for active dogs.

Once you have Tasha more dog-tired, you're ready to incorporate part two of my game plan — teaching her how to settle on cue. Work on this when she is already tired.

The *settle* signal rewards a dog for exhibiting calmness and quietness. You are reshaping her behavior by giving her frequent praise and an occasional food treat as encouragement. During quiet times, perhaps when you are watching television at night, put Tasha on a long lead. Step on one end. Whenever she plops down or sits quietly, wait a few seconds, then say *settle* and calmly hand over a treat. If she becomes excited, ignore her. Wait for her to quiet down again before rewarding with a treat. As she learns what is expected, gradually extend the time between your cue and her reward.

As you interact with Tasha, watch your energy response and tone of voice, too. You don't want to accidentally accelerate her actions. At night, try giving her a purposeful massage while you speak softly and calmly. Gently praise her for toning down her energy level and reward her for moments of quiet and calm behavior. Tasha sounds like a fun dog who definitely will never bore you!

Piddly Puddles

Q My best friend has three young adult miniature pinschers who don't seem to understand that their bathroom is outside. Her house has wall-to-wall carpet and when I visit, I am taken aback by the smell of urine. The dogs may be small but the smell is strong. My friend always apologizes and dismisses the severity of the problem by saying the puddles are small and cleanup is easy and quick. I've had dogs all my life and currently have a large poodle who lets me know when she must go outside. She never makes messes in my house. Any advice on how to help my friend?

A If I were to identify the primary negative trait of miniature pinschers, difficulty in house-training would top the list, though this trait applies to many toy breeds. Part of the problem is that tiny dogs physically just can't hold their bladders for as long as bigger dogs, but often the issue is that the owners don't insist on house-training as rigorously as they would with a large dog. Some people with small breeds such as Yorkshire terriers, pugs, min pins, and dachshunds worry about putting their precious pets out in cold or wet weather or may dismiss their messes as minor lapses and overlook them. But small piddles and poops still add up to a big problem that needs to be corrected, and all dogs need to learn that their bathroom is outside.

Unlike cats, dogs do not naturally house-train themselves — they all need help to learn proper bathroom habits. In your friend's case, she has not properly house-trained her min pin trio and her house is suffering the consequences. It's time for you to level with her about the odor in her home. Other guests to her house may not say anything to her but will be less likely to make return visits.

Offer to work with your friend and her dogs. Take her trio to the veterinary clinic to make sure they do not have any medical condition that may be causing them to have weak bladders. Most likely, however, they urinate indoors because they don't know the difference or they are each marking their own territory within the house with their signature scents. Male and female dogs will both display marking behavior, especially if they have not been neutered or spayed. Studies show a dramatic drop in this unwanted behavior following sterilization surgery.

PAW PRINTS
Chanda-Leah, a toy poodle, put her paw prints in history and made it into the *Guinness Book of World Records* for being able to perform the most tricks — 469 and counting.

Your friend must start from the beginning and completely retrain her dogs if she wants to solve this problem. Ask if she is amenable to crate training her trio or confining them to one room (like a kitchen or other room with an uncarpeted floor) when she can't be at home to supervise them. Establish a routine in which the dogs are ushered outside as soon as they wake up in the morning, after meals, after playtime, and before bed. Encourage your friend to praise each dog every time they do their business outside. If she catches a dog in the act inside, she should clap her hands loudly to startle and distract him long enough to grab him and take him outside. The minute he does go to the bathroom outside, she can heap on the praise and give a treat.

Accidents will happen during the training process, but it is important not to become angry or frustrated. When you vent those emotions, training stops and your dogs just become fearful or confused. It is futile, and foolish, to punish dogs when they do make puddles or defecate in the house. All they will learn is to do their business secretly or when their owner is not around.

Another step your friend must take is to thoroughly clean all her carpeting and furniture with an enzyme-based product that actually destroys the protein molecules in urine and feces and eliminates odor rather than covering it up with another smell. There are many pet cleanup products on the market that work this way. Do not use any products with ammonia, because it smells enough like urine to actually attract dogs back to the scenes of their crimes. When her dogs are thoroughly trained to go out only doors and not to have accidents in the house, it sounds as though she will need to replace a great deal of carpeting and padding. When she shops for new flooring, suggest that she consider pet-friendly types like tile or laminate!

Stop Begging, Cold Turkey

Q My seven-year-old cocker spaniels, Billy and Bessie, are champions at begging for food. They each take a position on either side of me at dinner. Every time I put a forkful in my mouth, I can feel two sets of brown eyes boring into me. They really work on me, and I end up succumbing to their begging and giving them a little bit of food from my plate. The problem is getting worse. They are now targeting my dinner guests, some of whom do not take kindly to dogs watching them eat. I want to stop this behavior, but is it too late?

A Who can resist those begging eyes? That slight drool and ever-so-subtle whimper for a piece of your meat-loaf or a spoonful of gravy? Billy and Bessie have learned that when people gather around the dining room table, lip-smacking goodies seem to fall from the sky. With such rewards, of course their begging behavior is increasing. Unfortunately, some charming beggars transform into thugs who aggressively try to take food from you. Others gain too much weight from nibbling on high-fat table food and become ideal candidates for diabetes, heart problems, arthritis, and other health problems. A little bit of leftover chicken or steak won't hurt, but it's important to limit their intake.

My father used to love pulling up to the drive-through window and ordering three cheeseburgers with all the fixings: two for himself and one for his dog Keesha. He stopped when Keesha became very ill with pancreatitis, a potentially fatal disease. My dad never conquered his own fast-food cravings, but he did make smarter food choices for Keesha after that. Whenever he munched on cheeseburgers in his car, she enjoyed a high-protein, low-fat dog treat from the glove compartment. She slimmed down and became healthier as a result.

As for your chowhound duo, it's never too late to break the begging habit. When you start your retraining regime, it may be easiest to usher them into another room when you have company, so you and your guests can dine in peace. Turn on a radio and give them treat balls with holes that they must nose around to make kibble and other goodies fall out. This makes them work for their treats and keeps them occupied while you enjoy your dinner.

> **BREED BYTE**
> The AKC accepts four specific colors for cocker spaniels: black, black with tan points, parti-colored, and ASCOB (Any Solid Color Other than Black).

When it's just the family, start new habits immediately by not giving food from your plate to Billy and Bessie. Completely ignore their pleas for food (after all, you know they are not starving). Expect their begging behavior to become worse before it improves, because they will think that if it worked before, more of the same will work again. Everyone at the table needs to ignore both dogs completely. Don't even look at them or tell them "no begging!" They need to learn that dogs should be neither seen nor heard at the table. If Billy and Bessie persist, then teach them to *down* and *stay* while the family is eating. This gives them something to do while you finish enjoying your meal.

You cannot succeed without enlisting the aid of your friends and family members. Explain that you do not wish to have Billy and Bessie fed from the table. Let them know that you're doing this out of concern for the health of your dogs and the comfort of your guests. If everyone at the table ignores the dogs (no eye contact, no talking, no petting — nothing!), they will eventually learn that begging no longer yields a reward and that the proper place for treats is in their bowls after the people leave the table.

Putting the Brakes on Chasing

Q I must keep a leash on Boomer, my terrier mix, when we take walks in the neighborhood and in our local park. Otherwise, if he spots a cat or squirrel, he takes off and no matter what I do, he doesn't stop. He does everything he can to catch these animals. So far, they've all managed to escape down a hole or up a tree before Boomer can reach them, but I'm afraid he will kill anything he catches. He not only runs away on our walks, he sometimes scoots out the front door when I answer the doorbell and chases a stray cat he sees through the picture window. How can I make him pay attention to me and leave other animals alone?

A Ah, the art of the chase. Most dogs will chase anything that runs, and terriers are particularly tuned to the hunt. Some animal behaviorists believe there is a genetic component to chasing. Once certain dogs detect movement, their eyes lock in, their predatory nature kicks in, and they charge. While many canines can't resist dogging cats or shadowing squirrels, others take on bigger prey and will scurry after skateboarders, run after runners, or chase cars, which can be embarrassing to the owner and dangerous for the dog.

Since cats and squirrels are Boomer's preferred prey, let's look at what's happening with him. Some dogs chase small animals for fun; others chase to kill. From both instinct and practice, many dogs know how to grab and shake a small animal all in one motion and break its spine. Identifying a playful chase as opposed to pure predatory instinct is not easy, and you definitely don't want to find out the hard way if Boomer is out for a romp or in for the kill. You need to stop his chasing behavior before he hurts a neighbor's pet or chases a squirrel right in front of a moving car.

Identify as many specifics as possible when Boomer bursts into chase mode. Pay attention to the time of day, the location, the object being chased, and his specific physical and verbal actions. The more details, the better you will be able to predict his reactions and intercede to curb the chase desire. By doing this doggy detective work, you can start to identify a predictable pattern in order to come up with an effective treatment plan.

When you walk in the neighborhood or park, do not feed Boomer his full meal before you go or, even better, wait to feed him until after you return from your walk. You want him a little hungry so he will pay more attention to you. Fasten a treat pouch with his favorite goodies around your waist. You must keep Boomer on a leash while he is learning to pay attention to you. Each time you spot a cat, squirrel, bird, or any moving target, reorient Boomer to look at you by telling him *watch me*. (See To Err is Human, page 153 for more on this cue.) Then have

him sit politely to earn a treat while he ignores these furry temptations. The goal is for Boomer to learn a new association. As he discovers that he gets a prized treat whenever he sees a cat, bird, or squirrel, he will look to you instead of speeding after these critters.

As for his bolting out the door, put him on a leash before you head for the door, especially if you can tell from his behavior that he has chasing on his mind. Always make him *sit* or *stay* before you allow him out the door. Do the same when you return from a walk so he gets the idea that he must stop and sit whenever he approaches a door. As he learns, practice leaving the door open for a few moments while he sits nicely (keep that leash on him, though!).

Throughout, please be patient, as the chase drive is very strong in terriers, and changing Boomer's behavior may take a lot of time and repeated commands. For dogs with strong chase drives, holding a *stay* is very challenging. With some dogs, the urge to chase is just too strong to trust them off-leash in areas with squirrels and cats.

In addition to teaching Boomer better self-control, I also recommend improving his recall so that he can chase after an acceptable object such as a tennis ball or dog toy. When he heeds your call to *come,* reward him by flinging the acceptable toy in different directions and encourage him to give chase.

Snakes and Snails and Puppy Dog Tails

Q My dogs, Fred and Ginger, are terrier mixes who enjoy off-leash romps and love to snoop around in the woods. I like letting them run free, but there are poisonous snakes in our area and I want to keep them safe. Is there any way to get them to stay away from snakes and other dangerous wild animals?

A The primary culprit behind dogs and snakebites is canine curiosity. Most dogs love to poke their noses in shrubs, thick grasses, and other spots that may harbor snakes, skunks, or other wild creatures not so wild about dogs. Even though some dogs are naturally afraid of snakes, others respond to the sight of a coiled rattler with intense interest or even aggression. If a snake ventures into their turf, some dogs will fight first and suffer the consequences later.

According to my friend Kelly Burch, who has successfully taught hundreds of dogs to just say no to snakes, training begins in an outdoor setting. In his classes, the dogs are fitted with a special collar that emits warning signals and then kept on leashes as the instructor shows them a live, defanged rattlesnake. When the dog gets near the snake, the trainer releases an electric pulse from the dog's collar that teaches the dogs to associate the snake with an unpleasant experience. That's important because dogs have a tendency to hear a sound and hurry to check it out. They risk getting bitten in the face if they rush in and come face to face with a startled, angry snake.

In addition to helping dogs stay away from snakes in any locale, from hiking trails to their own backyards, snake-avoidance training can save human lives. Snakes are hard to spot, and hikers sometimes don't see them until it is too late. A snake-trained dog with superior senses, however, can alert his human pals to stay away from places with snakes and avoid a potential accident.

TREATING SNAKEBITE IN DOGS

If your dog does get bitten by a snake, don't panic. The vast majority of venomous snake bites are not fatal to dogs, but you should seek medical care.

◆ Walk slowly back to your car, or carry your dog if possible. Excessive movement spreads the venom more quickly.

◆ A snakebite is often very painful and may cause the gentlest of dogs to bite, so do not handle the wound directly.

◆ Do not apply ice to the wound or apply a tourniquet or attempt to suck out the venom.

CANINE JOCKS RULE!

Do you share your home with a four-legged jock? Once you've laid down a foundation of basic obedience training, there are lots of organized sports activities for you and your dog to enjoy together. Here are a few to think about.

AGILITY. This sport appeals to dogs who love to conquer obstacle courses. Whether for fun or for competition, agility challenges dogs to wiggle through weave poles, jump through tires, climb up and down ramps and dash through tunnels. This sport is all about posting clean runs and quick times. Learn more about the various groups sponsoring agility events by visiting the Dog Patch Web site at www.dogpatch.org. Or visit the United States Dog Agility Association (USDAA), open to dogs of all sizes and breeds, at www.usdaa.com.

Another resource is the North American Dog Agility Council at www.nadac.org. Purebreds registered with the American Kennel Club can compete in AKC agility; find out more at www.akc.org.

FLYING DISCS. This sport caters to dogs who love to leap, chase, and snag plastic discs hurled into the air by their owners. Points are based on the distance and difficulty of the catch. Open to dogs of all breeds and mixes. For more details, contact the International Disc Dog Handlers' Association at www.iddha.com or the Skyhoundz Hyperflite Canine Disc World Championship at www.sky-houndz.com.

FLYBALL. Does your dog love to play tag and catch balls? Flyball may be his sport. Flyball is a relay race involving four-dog teams. Each dog zips down a lane, leaping over hurdles, to catch a launched tennis ball and race back to his starting point. The fastest team wins. To learn more, contact the North American Flyball Association at www.flyballdogs.com.

HERDING. Some dogs have built-in abilities to shepherd sheep, cattle, and other animals from Point A to Point B without bullying or harming the livestock. Learn more by visiting the American Herding Breed Association's Web site at www.ahba-herding.org.

LURE COURSING. For dogs with a strong chase drive, this sport uses an artificial lure connected to a long line strung around a series of pulleys. The lure zigzags around a course with points awarded based on a dog's speed and ability to follow it. More information is available at the American Sighthound Field Association Web site: www.asfa.org.

CANINE MUSICAL FREESTYLE. Love to dance with your dog? This sport spotlights human and dog partners performing choreographed moves to music. To learn more about this unusual activity, contact the Canine Freestyle Federation at www.canine-freestyle.org or the World Canine Freestyle Organization at www.worldcaninefreestyle.org.

PART V

Achieving Harmony at Home and Away

Your home should be your castle, not a palace of canine chaos. Who wants to enter the front door and be tackled by a blur of fur? Or cancel a date because your dog growls at your boyfriend? Or lose a good night's sleep because your poodle hogs the pillow? Yet when it comes to who actually spends the most time in our homes, dogs win paws down. No longer delegated to the backyard, most pet dogs are regarded as valued members of the family. Adding dogs to the mix of spouses, children, housemates, and other pets can make it a challenge to achieve harmony in your home.

Each person and each species needs to understand and honor the house rules to prevent snarling and snapping. Fortunately, dogs crave consistency and value hierarchy. They depend on us to teach them proper canine etiquette around babies, children, and houseguests. They look to us to learn if the sofa can be a comfy sanctuary or if it is off-limits. Our dogs can't contribute to paying the mortgage, but their presence in our lives can be a priceless pleasure if they know their place in the pack.

Paws de Deux

Q Laddie is a high-energy Border collie mix we adopted as a puppy about a year ago. We love him, but he wants to play with us constantly and he never seems to tire. If we ignore him, he grabs a toy and shoves it in front of our faces or drops it in our laps so we'll toss it for him to retrieve. We take him to the local dog park a couple of times a week where he zooms around and seems to enjoy himself.

We're thinking about getting a second dog in the hope of giving Laddie a playmate to romp with so that he doesn't demand so much of our attention. We've visited a few local animal shelters, but we want to know what we should look for in a second dog and how to properly introduce a new dog to our home.

A Border collies are notoriously energetic and active, so it's not surprising that Laddie is always on the go. You are right to provide him with suitable outlets like visits to a dog park, but once or twice a week won't cut it, especially for a dog this young and spirited. He needs a lot of exercise, including brisk walks, at least twice a day, that last 20 minutes or more.

The fact that Laddie enjoys dog parks is a good sign that he likes canine company. Use your dog park outings to scope out what type of dogs he seems to enjoy the most. Look for the dog's personality more than the breed.

Laddie would probably do best with a dog equal to his playful manner and high energy level.

Once you have narrowed down a list of three or four potential candidates at your local shelter, you're ready to test compatibility. Arrange a time at the shelter to bring Laddie to meet each dog one at a time. Many shelters provide meet-and-greet areas for just this purpose. Introductions need to be conducted on neutral turf, not at your home, to reduce the likelihood of Laddie eyeing the other dog as a territorial intruder.

Set yourself and Laddie up for success by bringing a dog-savvy friend or family member to assist you. You should each have a pocketful of tasty treats. Your goal is to make this an upbeat, positive event for both dogs. Take Laddie on his leash as your friend keeps the other dog on his leash. Speak in a happy voice and let the two dogs briefly do the "canine handshake" (sniffing each other's butts). Dogs are more likely to become aggressive if they are face to face, so avoid a head-on confrontation. After 10 seconds or so, separate the two dogs. Give them each a treat.

If the dogs behave, you're ready for the second step: taking them for a short walk. Position the dogs on the outside with you and your friend in the middle; don't let them wander too far in front of you at first. Continue talking to them in a positive voice. Stop occasionally, ask them to sit, and give them treats. Then continue walking. Periodically let them approach each other for an updated sniff. If they seem relaxed, you can give them some more room on the leashes, but be careful of tangles if they start to play. After a successful walk, let them loose together in an enclosed space, if one is available. Dogs often act very differently when leashed — many are actually better at making friends off-leash, because it is less confining.

During this introduction, pay close attention to each dog's posture. Good signs include play bowing, open mouths with relaxed facial muscles, and one acting submissive to the other (by lying down and exposing his belly for the other to sniff). Be wary if either dog bares his teeth, emits deep growls, stares directly, or assumes a stiff-legged stance. If this happens, see if you can diffuse the tension by calling the dog over to you, asking him to sit, and giving a treat. What you want is for the dog to abandon that aggressive posture and relax. If it works, you can let the dogs interact again, but a bit farther apart than the first time and for a briefer duration. If the dogs do not warm up to each other within a few minutes, this is not a good fit.

Once you do find a shelter dog that seems to get along with Laddie, it's time to see how they do at your home. Most shelters will agree to a trial period so that adoptive owners can make sure the new dog fits in with the family. Bring Laddie (and your friend) with you when you pick up the new dog, but separate them during the car ride home, preferably in their own crates. Once you arrive home, take them both out of the car on leashes. Walk them a bit and see how they act outside before bringing them inside your home. (Give them time to relieve themselves first!)

You need to support the resident, and therefore senior, dog in your home, so bring Laddie in before your friend enters with the shelter dog. This gives a clear signal to the new dog that Laddie, at least for now, is the top dog. Once they become pals and the new dog feels comfortable in your home, the true dominant dog will emerge. It may be Laddie or the shelter dog. Top dog is always greeted first, fed first, and allowed to lead the other on walks.

Do not let the two dogs be off-leash unsupervised until you are certain they get along. It might be a good idea to have another person accompany you on walks for the first few days, so that each dog has his own handler in case of problems. But from your description, Laddie sounds like a dog who will enjoy having a four-legged playmate.

Case of Canine Envy

Q I have a whippet, Greta, and a Border collie, Lex. Both are rescues whom I adopted last year within a couple of months of each another. Greta is about three and Lex is perhaps four years old. Whenever I rub Greta's belly or give her any special attention, Lex seems to appear out of nowhere and starts to paw at my arm or even lets out a slight growl at Greta. Is Lex acting jealous? How can I give Greta some one-on-one time without Lex butting in?

A You won't find envy in the canine dictionary, but the phrase "mine, mine, mine" certainly exists. Lex's behavior is triggered more by resource guarding than by jealousy over the attention Greta receives. Watch closely the next time Greta and Lex play with a toy and you can identify clear canine communication. Chances are that one will body block the other or lift an upper lip or make steady eye contact — signals that possession is nine-tenths of the law in the land of dogs. As hunters and pack animals, dogs have always demonstrated a "this is mine" attitude toward other canines when it comes to prized possessions, from the best part of the kill to a fuzzy chew toy.

When you rub Greta's belly, Lex steps in because he wants to guard the most valuable of all possessions — you.

Fortunately, Lex's actions are meant to seek your attention, not to harm Greta, and Greta has not retaliated by reacting territorially. Left unchecked, however, this attention-seeking behavior might escalate and lead to tension, and perhaps even fights and injuries.

Take the time to train both your dogs to ban this resource-guarding mentality. Consider enrolling in a basic obedience course or refresher training class with them. Make sure the class uses positive, reward-based methods. At home, all members of the household need to heed the same game plan. I hope that no one is yelling or physically punishing either dog, because these actions heighten levels of stress and anxiety.

It might be necessary for a while to separate the dogs when you want to devote individual time to each, by using doggy gates or putting one dog in a closed room or outside in a fenced backyard, but you should also teach Lex to *find your spot* whenever he approaches you when you are engaged in one-on-one time with Greta. (See Having Spot Find His Spot, page 178.) This command can keep a fight from occurring because you, as leader of the pack, are giving Lex an activity to perform. Toss Lex a treat to reinforce this preferred, compliant behavior.

Greta should also learn to wait quietly for attention in her own spot, but it is important to make sure you show Lex the same amount of attention so he doesn't feel that he needs to guard your time with him. By being consistant, you can teach both dogs to be patient.

THE ABCS OF CANINE INTRODUCTIONS

Most children love dogs and will rush up to pat a strange dog on the street or in a park. In many cases, the dog is happy to meet a new friend, but it is better to take it slowly and make sure the dog likes kids as much as the kids like the dog. Help children remember the proper way to greet a strange dog by reciting these ABCs.

ASK PERMISSION. Never run up to a dog. Check with his owner to see if the dog is friendly and if you can touch him.

BE SNIFFED. Give a dog time to check you out by slowly holding out your hand and letting him smell you before touching him. Don't stare right at him or bend over him — these actions can seem threatening.

CAREFULLY STROKE HIS BACK. Many dogs do not like to be patted on the head (many kids don't like this either!), though they might welcome a gentle scratch around the ears or under the chin.

Kids Dying for a Dog

Q Our kids have been bugging us to adopt a dog. My son is age seven and my daughter is nine. They promise they will feed, walk, and play with the dog. Are they old enough to be responsible in caring for a dog? My husband and I both work. Should we say yes or wait?

A Caring for dogs develops responsibility and self-esteem in growing children. I'm frequently approached by parents wondering if their children are too young or at the right age to adopt a dog. By age seven, in general, children are mature enough to recognize that dogs, just like people, have feelings and need kindness and care. The actual skills necessary to care for pets, though, depend more on a child's ability to take responsibility and exercise self-control than on an age group. I know some seven-year-olds who are extremely attentive and capable of feeding, watering, exercising, and playing appropriately with puppies and dogs. I know some immature twelve-year-olds who could not be relied on to feed a dog his daily meal even once.

You know your children's maturity levels. Spend some time with your spouse going over scenarios involving your children. Do they exercise proper caution by asking people if they can pet their dogs before bounding up to a dog? Do they complete their family chores on time? Do they take care of their toys? How do they act around pets belonging to friends and relatives?

You and your husband also need to ask questions of yourselves. Are you willing to take on the added responsibilities and costs (in terms of both time and money) of bringing a dog into the family? Are you willing to care for the dog when your children grow up and head for colleges or careers? Some dogs can live up to 18 years and longer. You could be caring for a senior dog with medical problems while your young adult children live hours away. Be candid with yourself and with each other.

Parents need to make canine caregiving an opportunity, not a punishment, for children. If your son doesn't do his homework or your daughter forgets to take the garbage out, don't punish them by telling them they must now walk the dog. Never make caring for the dog seem to be a burden or punishment to your children or they can develop resentment and anger and take it out on the dog.

Finally, round up your children for a family heart-to-heart talk. Remind them that dogs, unlike toys, are living, breathing animals with feelings. Then seek answers to the following questions:

◆ Why do you want a dog? Because you love dogs or because you think you'll look cool around your friends?

◆ Are you willing to attend dog-training classes?

◆ Will you help feed, water, and exercise your dog every day?

◆ Will you treat your dog with love and kindness even if he piddles on your carpet or chews your favorite book or accidentally scratches you when playing?

◆ Can you handle dog hair or drool on your favorite pair of black jeans?

◆ Will you bathe your dog and clean up after him?

◆ Can you respect that dogs sometime need to be left alone, especially when sleeping?

◆ Will you teach your dog commands and fun tricks?

◆ Will you obey leash laws when taking your dog out for walks?

Once you're satisfied with their responses, it is time to make this dog adoption truly a family affair. Teach children the right way to greet and respect the new family dog — and all dogs. Explain to them that when a dog tucks his tail, yelps, or tries to wiggle free from bear hugs, he wants some space. Point out that when a dog approaches them freely and stays by them, these are positive signs that the dog enjoys their company.

After you adopt a dog, set up a schedule that lists who is doing which chore/activity each week for the new family dog. Put this schedule in a prominent place, such as on the refrigerator door, for easy access to check off completed tasks. This schedule can reduce the chance of forgetting to feed the dog or taking him for a needed walk.

To ensure success, include your children in discussions on caring for your dog. Often, kids can offer great suggestions and be part of the solution when it comes to any behavior problems in your dog.

DOG BITE SAFETY

Doggone Safe (www.doggonesafe.com) is a nonprofit organization dedicated to preventing dog bites through education. According to the group, dog attacks are the number one public safety issue for children. In addition to The ABCs of Canine Introductions on page 211, kids should learn "to be a tree" when approached by a rowdy, threatening, or unfamiliar dog. This means stand perfectly still with your branches (arms) at your side and your eyes on your roots (feet). Stay in this position until the dog leaves or help arrives.

CHOOSING THE RIGHT DOG FOR A CHILD

Many of us are blessed with fond memories of our childhood dogs. I was lucky to grow up with Crackers, an overweight beagle, and Peppy, a high-energy Border collie mix. Crackers moved quickly only when she smelled a plateful of food. Peppy behaved like a canine bar bouncer, swiftly ushering away any dog who dared to step a paw on our property.

Any time you adopt a dog, especially if you have young children, it's vital to do your homework about various breeds. The diverse dog world includes itty-bitty canines like the Chihuahua and mountain-size ones like Saint Bernards. To a certain extent, purebreds possess particular temperaments — golden retrievers are accurately named for their sweet, sunny personalities. They usually love everybody, but there are exceptions. I've met bashful Jack Russell terriers and boisterous King Charles cavalier spaniels.

I tell you this so that you do not lock into a dog's breed as the sole indicator of temperament. Mixed breed dogs make wonderful pets also. Remember that environment plays a keen part, too, in how dogs act and react. Dogs, like people, fill their brains with memories: good and bad, happy and scary. What happens to them as puppies can influence how they react to similar scenarios as adults.

In a household with children and working parents where time is a precious commodity, my advice is to consider adopting a young adult dog instead of a puppy. A young adult dog will most likely have passed his chewing phase, and will be house trained and possibly have some basic obedience training. He will probably have received his puppy vaccinations and be neutered or spayed. Depending on the dog's personality and age, he could also be calmer than a high-spirited, active puppy.

If you are interested in a particular breed, I suggest contacting a breed rescue group or other dog group that fosters adoptable dogs in family homes. You will get more details on the dog's personality and how he or she reacts to home settings — kids, adults, other pets, and even the vacuum cleaner. Most come house-trained and, with any luck, are past the heavy-duty chewing puppy phase.

Clingy Canine

Q Our sweet but clingy Australian shepherd came to us from a breed rescue group about a month ago. Teddy follows us around the house like a shadow. Sometimes when we come home from work, we find that he has shredded a sofa pillow or stolen the sponge from the kitchen and chewed it up. He always rushes to greet us and seems very anxious. We feel terrible leaving him alone, but we can't stay home 24 hours a day to keep him company, and we can't keep him in a crate all day either. What can we do to help him feel more at home when he is there by himself?

A Two emotions are at work in your household: Teddy's separation anxiety and your feeling of guilt for having to bid him good-bye each morning and head to work. Guilt affects millions of hard-working dog owners who want to make their homes comfortable and secure for their stay-behind dogs. They feel bad about leaving the dog home alone, but of course they must go to their jobs and earn paychecks. The guilt surfaces when they make a big fuss over their dogs when they come home. Unfortunately, that approach can make dogs like Teddy more clingy and more in need of their attention.

The biggest problems with dogs who are bored or anxious about being left at home include inappropriate elimination, incessant barking, and chewing up household items. Some dogs pace around in a panic or claw at windows and doors. Certain facts you cannot change — unless you win mega-millions in the lottery and can suddenly quit your job! Your dog spends more time inside your home than you do. But you can shed guilt-laden thoughts by designating a safe, cozy spot for Teddy to hang out in during the day and by giving him something fun to do in your absence. It is also important to avoid a common bad habit among working owners: making a big deal out of leaving and returning to your house.

Start by rescripting your comings and goings. Some owners unintentionally create separation anxiety in their dogs because they make a big deal of departures ("I'm so sorry I

BREED BYTE
Australian shepherds are touted for their ability to herd sheep and cattle, but the breed did not originate in the land down under. It actually got its start in California in the mid-19th century.

have to go work today, Max, you poor thing") or arrivals ("Hey, Max! Guess who's home? Where's my sloppy kiss?"). For Teddy's sake, cease the emotion-filled departures and arrivals. Exit and enter without a lot of fanfare. Give him a treat or activity before you walk calmly out the door, but don't make a fuss about leaving. When you return, say hello, but then spend several minutes checking your mail or listening to your phone messages before making a fuss over him. You are teaching him that it isn't a big production when you leave and return and that he must wait patiently for your undivided attention.

Here are a few other strategies to turn your home into a haven for Teddy during your absence.

- ◆ **LIMIT HIS ACCESS.** You're right not to crate your dog if you are gone for more than four or five hours at a time. That is far too taxing for any canine bladder or patience. Instead, identify a room in your home where you can close a door or use doggy gates to keep Teddy safely inside. These small places often give dogs like Teddy a feeling of security and may help him to calm down.

- ◆ **BRING ON THE FOOD FEAST.** A few minutes before you head out the door for work, give Teddy a hollow, hard rubber toy stuffed with his favorite treat: peanut butter, cream cheese, mashed bananas, pieces of rice cake, or pieces of kibble. Your dog should be so happily working to release every little morsel that he won't notice your absence for hours. This tactic can help curb destructiveness, overeager greeting, and separation anxiety tendencies. Clean these rubber toys in your dishwasher or hot, soapy water at least once a week.

◆ **THOROUGHLY DOG PROOF** any room where he will be spending time alone. Provide him with a comfy bed, a couple of favorite toys, and a bowl of water.

◆ **TURN ON THE TELEVISION** or radio to provide some sound to counter the silence.

◆ **VARY THE DAILY ROUTINE.** If he likes other dogs, treat Teddy to an occasional day at a doggy day care center or a midday visit from a dog-friendly neighbor or a professional pet sitter. (See Choosing a Good Day Care, page 238–239.)

◆ **GIVE HIM PLENTY OF EXERCISE.** A tired dog is a more relaxed dog.

Remember not to make a big deal of leaving or returning so you do not feed into Teddy's insecurity. He is still a newcomer to your household and is learning that he can trust you to come home every day. It won't be long before he feels like a full-fledged member of the family.

DOES YOUR DOG NEED DRUGS?

Some dogs develop destructive behaviors such as breaking through windows, chewing holes in walls, and destroying sofas in their frantic efforts to cope with feelings of abandonment. Dogs with serious separation anxiety issues may need medication as well as behavior modification help from a professional dog behaviorist.

Look for a board-certified veterinary behaviorist (ACVB) or certified applied animal behaviorist. Ask for references from clients. You need solid guidance from someone properly trained to assist you and your dog.

Some behavioral medications can take several weeks to take effect. Although generally not addictive, efforts should be made to gradually wean a dog off a drug once he is able to maintain his behavior with reduced doses and effective behavior modification. Some dogs may need to be on medication for their entire lives, while others can function quite well on doses slowly reduced over time.

Training Can Be Child's Play

Q We're planning on enrolling in a basic obedience class for our young Border collie, Barney, and we hope to continue with clicker training and agility classes. My 10-year-old son is very interested in teaching Barney tricks. Is he too young to participate in the training classes with me? Will Barney respect him enough to obey him?

A Many professional dog trainers report that their best students are children and teenagers. It makes sense. Children and puppies possess wonderful young minds that soak up learning like sponges. In dog training classes, children learn success. They gain confidence by being able to show off tricks they taught their dog to their friends. It's definitely a win-win for dogs and for kids.

Children between the ages of nine and fifteen make the best students because they are the most open to learning. Adults often have too many bad habits to break or they become too goal-oriented. Trainers remark that it can be challenging to show adult students a new way to teach *sit* and *down*. The competitive nature also surfaces sometimes in classes with some adults wanting their dogs not only to learn the commands but also to be the best. That puts undue pressure on a dog and can interfere with effective training.

Another plus for young students: great eye–hand coordination and timing. In clicker training, you learn to press a small metal device to make a clicking sound each time your dog does the right step. You immediately follow that sound with a small treat to reinforce his actions. The timing of the click is essential. Adults may be a little slow with the clicking sound, but children possess good eye–hand coordination, thanks in part to their video game skills. They usually manage to click on cue.

I know a nine year old named Kim who enrolled in a clicker-training puppy class with her dachshund puppy, Bogart. The trainer in charge told me that Kim ranked top in her class, which included mostly adults. Kim even surprised her mom by getting Bogart to heed basic commands like *sit, stay,* and *settle* during the first day of clicker-training class. Now Kim and Bogart have advanced to work on new commands and fun tricks, and their confidence levels rise with each success.

Your children represent the next generation of the pet-loving public, so encourage them to join you in your dog's training classes. Then sit back and witness the maturity growth in both your children and your dog.

And Baby Makes Four

Q My husband and I jokingly refer to Samson as our first child. We adopted him from a greyhound rescue organization two years ago; he is now four. Samson is sweet, gentle, and charming with people. I just found out that I'm pregnant. We're excited about having a baby, but what should we do to prepare Samson for the new arrival? We don't want him to be jealous or upset when the baby comes.

A Congratulations on becoming a parent — again! Samson's sweet temperament should make for an easy transition upon the arrival of your baby. Still, he will surely be curious, and while a dog won't feel jealous the way an older sibling might, he may feel that he must compete with this new addition for your time and attention.

Start now to prepare Samson by gradually spending less one-on-one time with him. This is not meant to be unkind, but to help him cope with your need to devote a lot of time and energy to caring for your baby. If you are Samson's primary caregiver, have your husband take over some of those duties. You want Samson to continue to feel that he is a loved and vital member of the family but not that he is the central focus of your attention. You also don't want him to feel neglected.

Before the baby arrives, introduce Samson to as many other infants and toddlers as possible. Invite friends who have babies to visit so that Samson becomes accustomed to little ones in the house. Take him for walks near playgrounds or schools. Play tapes or videos of babies and children. Look for any opportunity to expose Samson to the sights, sounds, and smells of the baby world: crying, babbling, diaper changing, strollers, and so forth. You're building him a baby database that he can download when your baby comes home.

Of course, it is very important that you closely supervise his interaction with all babies and children. Reward him for gentle behavior and correct him if he is too nosy or if he tries to lick them. Teach him to sit politely to be petted. Be aware that sight hounds might chase and knock down running children, whose erratic motion and high-pitched voices can trigger chasing instincts. Don't take the chance of your children getting accidentally injured or bitten by a dog who becomes overly excited.

Silly as it sounds, I recommend that you carry a baby doll around with you when you walk Samson and when you relax or watch television. Get a recording of baby sounds and play it. A friend of mine even sprinkled baby powder on her forearm and baby food on her fingers to get her dog used to the smells.

Before you bring the baby home, ask your husband or a friend to bring home a blanket or other object that smells of your baby for Samson to sniff and become familiar with. When you come home, make the first introduction a rewarding one. Enter the house alone and give Samson a happy greeting and treat. Then have your husband follow you inside with your baby. Give Samson plenty of time to sniff and look over the baby while you keep a close watch on them.

Your life is about to change drastically, and many of your usual routines will be altered or gone forever. However busy you are, though, try to spend some quality solo time each day with Samson — even just a few minutes will help him feel secure. No matter how much you trust him, however, always supervise him when he is with the baby. With careful preparation and continued attention, Samson should quickly learn to accept this new addition to the pack and still feel loved by you and your husband.

BREED BYTE

Being around a greyhound with a white spot on her forehead brings good fortune, according to an old superstition. You may have better luck buying a lottery ticket if you want mega-dollars, but your dog is, of course, priceless.

Peter and Ugh, the Pee-Minded Pugs

SALLY HAD RECENTLY RELOCATED to a small second-story condominium with four pugs and two cats. Since the move, her two male dogs, Ugh, five years old, and Peter, one year old, had started fighting with one another, lifting their legs on furniture, and even defecating on the floor, something they had not been doing in their old home.

The dogs were walked three times a day, but Ugh in particular would hold his urine and wait to release it inside the condo. Frustrated, Sally realized she needed professional help. To rule out any possible medical condition such as a urinary tract or bladder infection, I conducted complete physical exams. Both dogs were deemed healthy. In taking their histories, I learned that Sally had adopted Ugh from a rescue group when he was about a year old and had purchased Peter three years later as a small pup from a breeder. This appeared to be a situation in which both males were trying to establish territory in the new home.

The first step in fixing this problem was for Sally to thoroughly clean her furniture and carpets with a commercial odor neutralizer that breaks down and removes odors rather than masking them. I put both dogs on a behavioral medication to address possible anxiety caused by the move. I also instructed Sally to stop giving Ugh and Peter table food and to discontinue free feeding in order to establish her leadership role. To discourage repeat episodes, their food bowls were repositioned at places where they had previously marked. To redirect their behavior, the two pugs needed a training tuneup. Any affection was to be initiated by Sally, not demanded by Ugh or Peter. Sally also had to enforce the *sit, stay, come,* and *off* commands. The dogs were no longer allowed on the sofa, both because it had become a place for inappropriate elimination and because it was possibly giving them the sense that they were as high in the social order as Sally was. Booby traps on the cushions (aluminum foil or plastic carpet runners with knobby side up) kept them off it.

When Sally was at home, the dogs were kept on long draglines attached to her or to non-movable furniture to control their movement in the house. When she was out, they were separated and placed in crates or gated rooms. I advised her to play therapeutic harp music and use an electric plugin to diffuse a calming pheromone to calm them down when they were left alone.

Within a few months, we were able to reduce the dosage of the behavioral medication. Acting calmer and more secure, both pugs stopped urinating and fighting in the condo and remembered to take their bathroom needs outdoors.

Contributed by Patrick Melese, DVM

Small Digs, Big Dog

Q I live on the 10th floor of a high-rise building in New York City. My one-bedroom condo is 600 square feet. I love city life and don't plan to move, but I really want to adopt a dog. I volunteer at a doggy day care on Saturdays, and I know that I could offer a deserving dog a good home. I prefer larger dogs who weigh at least 50 pounds. Would living in such a small space drive a big dog crazy?

A By all means, adopt a big lovable dog, but choose carefully. Physical size does not necessarily parallel the amount of energy a dog possesses. Some of the top canine couch loungers include greyhounds and Great Danes. Conversely, some dogs that turn into interior designers of the worst kind (chewing rugs and shredding sofas, all the while yapping nonstop) weigh in at less than 15 pounds.

Before you take any steps toward adopting, though, check with your condo association and learn their pet rules. Savvy condo groups focus on temperament — not poundage — in their pet policies. They want well-behaved dogs and responsible owners. Your next step should be to honestly assess how much time you have to exercise a dog and then be careful to choose a canine companion that will be satisfied with what you provide. In other words, if you can walk a dog twice a day for only 15 minutes, don't get a high-energy breed that needs lots of exercise. Great Danes, for example, may be big, but they are not typically shoving a leash in your lap and beckoning you to the door to run a marathon every day.

Dogs are very adaptable, and city dogs are exposed to many sights, sounds, and smells. These exposures usually enhance their social skills when they meet people and other critters during daily walks. Most big cities offer numerous canine amenities like doggy spas, bakeries, day cares, training centers, and dog-friendly transportation. When I was in New York with Chipper, she sat so nicely next to me that we had no trouble flagging down taxis. A few cabbies even remarked that Chipper showed more manners than some of their two-legged riders!

Big cities also provide plenty of places for dogs to get exercise. Seek out dog-friendly parks and canine play groups. If you work all day, look into a dog day care or hire a professional dog walker to give your dog a break in the middle of the day. Don't let the size of your place keep you from teaching your dog city manners. Keep plenty of treats in your tiny kitchen and work on commands like *sit pretty* (ideal when sharing elevators with dog-apprehensive strangers) and *curb* (stopping and sitting at intersections until the light turns green). Your dog will be happy to demonstrate his repertoire of tricks during walks and perhaps the two of you will convert more New Yorkers into dog fans. And don't forget to scoop your poop!

Bowser Hates Boyfriend

Q Can dogs be jealous of people? Rusty, my 40-pound mixed breed, loves other dogs and is even kind to cats. He is about five years old, and I got him when he was just a pup from a local animal shelter. He is well trained and greets everyone at my house in a friendly manner — except for my boyfriend. When my boyfriend and I are on the sofa, Rusty tries to sit between us. Rusty sleeps at the foot of my bed, but growls a little when my boyfriend spends the night. He hasn't bitten or attacked, but sometimes I catch him staring at my boyfriend. It makes my boyfriend a bit nervous. He hasn't been around dogs much. I really like this guy and we're talking about getting married. What can I do to get Rusty to be friendlier?

A Dogs do not get jealous in the human sense, but they can become protective of the members of their pack and will compete for attention from and proximity to their leaders. In this case, that's you. They are also very hierarchical, and from Rusty's perspective, the order of the pack is you, him, and then your boyfriend, the most recent addition. Rusty can undoubtedly detect your boyfriend's nervousness, which fuels his in-charge behavior even more and explains why he pushes between you on the sofa and growls at your boyfriend at bedtime. Just like a

toddler, Rusty has discovered that his canine antics focus your attention on him. Even if you reprimand him, negative attention is better than none in his mind.

Dogs can become overly attached to a single person, so it's good that Rusty is friendly toward others and heeds your obedience commands. Now you need to teach him to extend that pleasant behavior to your boyfriend. Rusty must also learn that while he has a new place in the hierarchy, he can still feel secure in his pack. To succeed, your boyfriend must cooperate with you to elevate his status to Number Two. When he visits, have him feed Rusty, first telling the dog to *sit*. When the three of you are entering or exiting the house, make sure that your boyfriend goes through the door before Rusty does. When you are on the sofa, have your boyfriend lead Rusty over to his dog bed and offer him a chew toy to keep busy. If you don't mind sharing the sofa with Rusty, make him settle down on his own end, not between you.

Hand the leash over to your boyfriend when you take Rusty for a walk. Ask him to tell Rusty to perform various behaviors on the walk, with the cues spoken in a calm, clear tone. Give your boyfriend a pocketful of treats to reward compliance. Eventually you can have him take Rusty out on his own, perhaps in an unfamiliar area where Rusty has to rely on your boyfriend for guidance and security. If your boyfriend is the real deal, he should be happy to engage in some play time with Rusty, such as tossing a ball or even playing a fun game of hide-and-seek in your house.

At bedtime, do not ban Rusty from your room. That has been his den since puppy days. However, he does need his own bed. You and your boyfriend need to make this doggy bed appear to be higher in real estate value than your bed. Do this by directing Rusty to a comfortable dog bed or a crate. Put treats or a special chew toy on the bed or in the crate. Tell Rusty to *lie down* and *stay*. Reward him with a treat. If he heads for your bed, toss a treat on his own bed. Praise him when he stays on his bed or inside his crate. The goal is to make Rusty view his bed or his crate as his personal bedroom. (You might need to experiment with a few different kinds of beds to find one that appeals to him.)

It will take some time for Rusty to realize that your boyfriend deserves his respect, so celebrate each small victory. By the time you are ready to exchange "I dos," Rusty may happily serve as ring bearer at your ceremony.

Dial "D" for Doggy Day Care

Q Lately, I've found myself spending more and more time at my job. I used to leave home at 7 A.M. and return at 5 P.M., but recently I haven't been coming home until around 7 P.M. I share my home with my wonderful dog, Murphy. He is four years old and well behaved. He likes other dogs and loves helping me entertain when we have company. He has access to a dog door leading to an enclosed area in my side yard to use as a bathroom area, and I leave him with toys and snacks and water. When I walk in the door, Murphy is ready to play, but I am exhausted. I feel guilty that I can't give him the attention and exercise he deserves. He is beginning to chew my belongings and beg for constant attention at night. What can I do?

A Guilt is a human emotion, not a canine one. I came up with the acronym "Great, Useful, Intelligent, Loving Tactics" for working out solutions to problems like juggling a demanding job and a young, playful dog. You already recognize that you're exhausted and your dog is frustrated. Murphy sounds like a sweet dog who enjoys your company, but you are right to be worried that he needs more attention. You've done a good job in providing him with the basic amenities, but the 12-hour days are cutting into quality time for you and Murphy and reducing his opportunities to exercise.

One suggestion is that you treat Murphy to doggy day care a couple of days a week. Many places offer quality care with hours that match your schedule. Don't let the price dissuade you. A young, energetic dog left home alone all day can start to display signs of loneliness and boredom, including destructive chewing, nonstop barking, and inappropriate urination. Correcting these bad behaviors and repairing the damage done by the dog can cost you more time and money (and much more frustration) than you will pay for day care. Murphy will enjoy unleashing his pent-up energy and hanging out with canine pals. At the end of the workday, you will pick up a tired, happy dog, not one who's been eagerly awaiting your return all day and is dying to play. You can come home and relax with your dog before heading for bed. You both win.

Another option is to hire a trusty teen or retiree in your neighborhood to come in the afternoons and give Murphy a good long walk and some attention. Or perhaps a nearby friend with a dog would bring Murphy along for a walk while you're at work if you offer to take the two dogs on longer treks on the weekends. Once Murphy is getting more exercise, he should start feeling less anxious and restless.

CHOOSING A GOOD DAY CARE

In deciding which doggy day care is best for your dog, ask your canine-owning friends to tell you what they like and don't like about area facilities. If there are several choices, narrow down your list to the most appealing ones and call to schedule a visit — alone. Taking your dog on your initial visit will only distract you and keep you from conducting an objective visit.

At each doggy day care, follow this checklist.

TAKE A COMPLETE TOUR OF THE CENTER. Staff members at quality centers are happy to show prospective clients where dogs play, lounge, and rest. Scratch off centers where staff members refuse to show the entire place.

SIZE UP THE FACILITY. Look at the number and size of dogs and determine if the space allocated is adequate or too small. Make sure the center offers a safe, enclosed outdoor area.

ASK ABOUT THE RATIO OF STAFF TO DOGS. Well-run establishments should have one employee for every four to six dogs. Dogs should never be left unsupervised.

CHECK FOR CLEANLINESS. Accidents happen, but good centers quickly clean up messes. Use your ears and nose, too. You shouldn't be deafened by the sound of noisy barking, and the place should smell fresh and clean.

REVIEW THE ADMISSION POLICY. Responsible centers require that all doggy guests be up-to-date on their vaccinations, be on regular flea and tick maintenance programs, be spayed or neutered, and be nonaggressive.

Once you've chosen a place, pay close attention to your dog's reaction to attending doggy day care. If he enjoys his time there, he will show his excitement by ushering you to the door when he is dropped off, not resisting and yanking the leash in the opposite direction. He should be happy to see you when you pick him up at the end of the workday but not desperate to leave or acting anxious and nervous.

Case of the Shrinking Bed

Q I live in a small town and have three big dogs that range in weight from 85 to 160 pounds. One drools. They are all males, ages three to six. They are very sweet, but their physical size seems to scare off potential boyfriends — that and the fact that I allow all three to sleep on my queen-sized bed at night. Obviously, there is very little room for even me to sleep. How can I find a great mate who isn't intimidated — or turned off — by my canine trio? How can I get my canine trio to accept a serious boyfriend into my bedroom?

A Sounds like you want a guy who loves dogs but doesn't act like one! Use the fact that you love your three dogs to your advantage in the dating game. Surveys show that people who own dogs are perceived as nicer and kinder than those who don't.

You have several options. Consider joining the growing number of pet-friendly online dating services. Hang out at your local dog park and strike up conversations with guys. Offer to volunteer at a fund-raising event for a local shelter or rescue group. Look for a "yappy hour" in your area (but take only one dog at a time!). The key to finding a guy who shares your love for dogs is to be honest. Let guys know right up front that you share your home with three large dogs. In searching for a mate, don't sacrifice your beliefs and certainly don't dismiss the needs of your dogs. Steer

DATING GOES TO THE DOGS

The world is changing rapidly, and a sign of the times is that pets are commanding more attention in many human relationships. About 62 percent of U.S. households have pets. Of those, about 40 million are single people. There are Web sites for people with pets looking for mates who have pets or who at least like them. A national survey recently conducted by a leading pet product manufacturer reported that a majority of people would stop dating someone who didn't like their dog or whom their dog didn't like.

clear of any guy who tells you to decide between him and your dogs. Those "me or else" guys aren't worth your time or energy.

By the way, given the sheer size of your canine pals, I strongly recommend you provide them with their own beds in your bedroom and retrain them to sleep there instead. Pets are definitely one of those environmental factors such as sound, temperature, humidity, light, and movement that contribute to poor sleep. Researchers at the Mayo Clinic Sleep Disorders Center have discovered that about half the people who let pets share their bed at night suffer from disrupted sleep that results in being tired each morning. Initially you may need to tether them safely to a heavy piece of furniture with their leashes so that they cannot physically reach your bed.

As for introducing another human to your room, make sure your canine trio meet your boyfriend outside the bedroom first. Let them spend some time getting treats from him and playing with him. They need to build a bond with him that will strengthen the trust to feel okay about him being in any room in your house.

Poodle Hogs Pillow

Q My poodle, Precious, earns her name, at least during daylight hours. She is sweet, gentle, and always ready to learn new tricks. My problem is that she turns into a pillow pig at night. She starts out by putting her head on the edge of my pillow but by the middle of the night, she has taken over half or more. Her activity wakes me up. Sometimes she presses her cold wet nose against my neck or emits little yips when she is deep in dreamland. I want her to sleep on my bed, but how can I keep her off my pillow so I can get some sleep?

A When it comes to sharing your bed with your dog, you're not alone. In fact, about a third of today's dog owners sleep with their pets, an arrangement that dates back hundreds of years. The Mexican hairless breed, also known as the Xoloitzcuintli, was valued by pre-Aztec Mexicans as a bed warmer and companion. The term "three-dog night" originated with Eskimo tribes in Alaska who added sled dogs as bed warmers based on the temperature. The colder the night, the more dogs they invited in to keep their toes toasty.

Precious sounds like one bossy poodle. She has decided that bedtime entitles her to sleep wherever she chooses, regardless of your preferences. Cute as she may be, you need to regain control of your bed, not only to enjoy a sound sleep but also to remind Precious who calls the shots in your home. You are fortunate that she has not become territorial about bedtime turf. Some dogs who view themselves as top dogs in the family will growl or even nip their human bedmates who dare to toss and turn at night.

It's time to teach Precious that although she is welcome on your bed, you are the one who determines where she sleeps. Make her sit and wait until you call her up. Direct her to the foot of your bed and provide her with her own

pillow or special blanket. If she ventures north toward your pillow, move her back to the foot of the bed. Once she is there, praise her. It may take a few nights before Precious learns your new bedtime rules, but eventually, she will roost in her own spot and let you enjoy a full night's sleep without a pillow fight.

My Mom's Dog Hates Me

Q My mother, who lives in a different state, owns an Italian greyhound named Maggie who seems to hate me. I admit I don't like her very much either. She acts very upset when I visit. She won't let me pet her and avoids me, staying very close to my mom. If Maggie gets the chance, she defecates on my clean clothes in my open suitcase. If I drop towels on the floor in the bathroom, she urinates on them. Why does she hate me, and what can we do to change her attitude? Her behavior is ruining my visits.

A It sounds like Maggie is very closely bonded to your mom and not used to visitors. Often when a dog and her owner live alone, the dog becomes wary of outsiders. I imagine that your mom doesn't get too many overnight visitors, or even daytime guests. If Maggie doesn't leave the house much, your mother is her entire world and she has become too dependent on a single person for attention, which makes her suspicious of others.

Because Maggie is poorly socialized, she sees you as a threat and is acting out by marking her territory every chance she gets. Urinating and defecating on your property is her way of saying, "This is *my* house and *my* mom, and don't you forget it." She doesn't hate you. She simply becomes anxious when you invade her territory.

A lot of the work required to help Maggie over this attitude will fall on your mom. She needs to start taking Maggie places to help socialize her and accustom her to strangers. If your mom has friends who like dogs, she should take Maggie on social visits to their homes. To set up Maggie for success, the initial visits must be short and pleasant. Your mom should bring Maggie's favorite snacks, whatever they are, or even introduce a delicious new treat like pieces of hot dog or cheese — anything that makes her really pay attention and associate new experiences with great rewards. Maggie will be afraid at first, so the enticements need to be special.

Your mom's friends can make a fuss over Maggie when she visits. Chances are Maggie will be shy around them, so they shouldn't force themselves on her physically by bending over her, making eye contact, or trying to pet her. They can talk to her in a happy voice, however, and offer her treats from their hand. If she is very nervous in the beginning, they should ignore her and just drop treats near her so she isn't overwhelmed. In time, Maggie will start to realize that strangers are a source of kind words and good treats and are not to be feared.

Once Maggie shows some appropriate social skills out of the house, the next hurdle involves turning your mom's home into a welcoming place. Your mother should start inviting people over to her house specifically to visit Maggie. Visitors should offer Maggie treats when they are there and talk to her in an upbeat tone. Again, after a number of enjoyable interactions, the dog will start to see visitors as a pleasure rather than a threat.

As for your relationship with Maggie, you need to walk in with a new attitude — a genuine desire to make friends. When you first go into the house, act happy to see Maggie and offer her some of the special treats that she's been receiving from other people. If your mom has been working on this, Maggie shouldn't be too stressed when she sees you and should readily take the food. Ask your mom if you can take over the mealtime duties and daily walks with Maggie while you are there. What you are doing is communicating a leadership role and showing Maggie that her place in the pack comes after you, but that you can provide comfort and security.

When you go to the room where you sleep when you visit, put some of Maggie's treats around in strategic places. Lay the treats on your suitcase and around the bed. Let Maggie come into the room and discover the treats. Do the same thing in the guest bathroom. Feed her some treats from your hand in these rooms, too (but still remember to keep the doors closed when you're not there to supervise her). Don't rush into petting her — look for a more relaxed attitude and maybe even a tail wag first.

The goal here is to change Maggie's view of you and visitors in general from an intrusion to a welcome diversion. Food is a great way to do this, along with gentle behavior and talking. It's amazing how quickly a dog's opinion of someone can change when a particularly good treat is offered or a favorite game is initiated!

Mine, Mine, All Mine

Q Our Boston terrier, Foggy, has started to growl and snap at our cats whenever they come within 10 feet of his food bowl, even if it is empty. Recently, he lunged at one of them, making her climb up a cat tree to escape. He also stares icily at my husband and me when we walk by his bowl. Foggy is nine months old and neutered. When the food bowl isn't involved, he is fun and friendly and obedient. Why is he guarding his food bowl with such intensity?

A Foggy doesn't hold the deed to your house or the title to your car, but he does know the concept of ownership. From his viewpoint, the food bowl — empty or full — is one of his most prized possessions and, even if they show no interest in it, he must ensure that cats or people don't attempt to steal his bowl. This common type of resource guarding harks back to his ancestors' need to protect food and other resources in order to survive. Snapping and growling at other members of the pack was a way for dogs to tell them to back off and leave their food alone. Despite being domesticated, some modern-day dogs extend this territorial thinking to favorite toys, bedding, and even a certain location in the house, like a sunny spot near a window.

At nine months, Foggy is also beginning to feel more grown-up, and like all young adults, he is testing the limits of authority. He wants to know if he can chase you away from his bowl and if the cats will yield to his threats. From your description, Foggy's turf defending is growing in intensity and range. Unchecked, this behavior can become dangerous, with Foggy escalating from growls to snapping, even to biting. As natural as it may seem, do not yell at Foggy or physically punish him for guarding his food bowl. You risk making the problem worse: He will feel a greater need to protect his bowl since it will appear to him that you are angry enough to fight for it.

This problem did not surface overnight, and it won't go away in one day. Stopping resource guarding takes time.

The first step is to establish a new dinnertime protocol. You and your husband must call the shots at meals. Your goal is to teach Foggy that positive experiences occur when people approach his bowl and that you reign as the Keeper of Great Chow, worthy of his respect.

Do not let Foggy be a free feeder who nibbles all day. Take his bowl away between meals and store it out of sight. During your retraining period, bring out not one but two food bowls — one empty and one containing food. Call the dog to a new feeding place that isn't a high-traffic area in your home. Moving the bowl into different locations in your home will reduce Foggy's territorial tendencies.

Place the bowls on a counter or shelf out of his reach. Ask Foggy to *sit* and *stay* and then put down the empty bowl. (Watch the surprised look on his face!) Then drop a piece of food into the empty bowl on the ground. Do not bend over. Wait until he eats that piece before dropping another. If he shows no protectiveness, try putting a few pieces of food in your hand and invite him to take them.

Alternate between dropping food in his bowl and hand-feeding him. When he starts to eat from his bowl, drop more pieces into it. Once in a while, drop in a "jackpot treat" like a piece of chicken or steak, something much tastier than his regular dog food. It may take several meals before he accepts this new method of dining.

Once Foggy shows no signs of tension, you're ready for the next phase. Partially fill one bowl with his food and place it on the floor. Call Foggy and again have him *sit* and *stay* before you give him the *okay* sign to approach his food bowl. The goal is to make him work for his food. As he starts to eat, place a second bowl with some premium food about 10 feet away. Call him over to this bowl. As he starts to eat from the second bowl, go back to the first bowl and add special treats to up its food value before you call Foggy over. Continue switching between bowls until he has finished his meal, then take them away and hide them.

Over a few weeks, gradually move the two bowls closer together as you feed him. You need to watch Foggy's reactions to determine how quickly you can merge the two bowls. He should be displaying a relaxed body posture. This dual-bowl tactic is designed to build positive associations and increase Foggy's trust that you, or other people, make feeding time fun and exciting, not tense and upsetting. You are using positive reinforcement rather than threats or physical force to show Foggy that food time is not a time to fight. He is learning that by giving up a resource, he is rewarded with something even better. Eventually, you will be able to present him with a single bowl, though he should always be expected to sit and wait for your signal before eating.

I followed these steps with my corgi, Jazz, and within a couple of weeks his guarding behavior disappeared. We turned mealtime into a fun game of doggy dining etiquette. He would happily leap into a *sit* position, watch me put down the bowl, heed my *wait* cue and my *watch me* cue before approaching his bowl once I gave the *okay* sign. I was able to pet his back while he ate, praising him. It worked, and it can work for you and Foggy.

If you don't feel that you can stop Foggy on your own, however, I urge you to seek help from a professional animal behaviorist. This is a serious behavior problem that can eventually threaten the safety of you, your family and visitors, and your cats.

Ruff! Ruff! Road Trip!

Q All I have to do is say the words "car ride" and my Labrador retriever gets giddy with excitement and starts dancing around. I enjoy taking him along when I go on errands and when I visit family and friends out of town. He absolutely loves to ride in the front seat and stick his head out the window. Why do so many dogs like to do this? Also, I'm a conscientious driver, but is there anything I can do to make life on the road with my dog safer?

A Be happy that he isn't begging for the keys like a teenager or whistling at that cute poodle in the BMW convertible next to you at the intersection! Many dogs love car rides, partly because they love to go with us wherever we go. Another reason is that they exist in a world of smells. Their nose acts as a steering wheel, directing them from one great odor to the next. As they whiz along with their heads out the window, dogs are gathering a wealth of information about the passing world. Road trips also help hone canine socialization skills by exposing dogs to new and different sights, sounds, and, most important, smells with each passing mile.

Chipper also loves car trips, and although I used to allow her to stick her head out the window to better enjoy the ride, this is not safe. Even traveling around town at lower speeds exposes dogs to the risk of eye injuries from flying debris. There is also the chance that something will tempt a dog to leap out of a moving car, which is a good reason to open the windows only a few inches. And all it takes is a sudden stop for your dog to become a projectile inside your car, possibly injuring you both.

As much as we might enjoy their company in the front seat, dogs are safer sitting in the back, where they can't distract the driver and won't be injured by the airbags in an accident. Just as there are car seats for infants and toddlers and seat belts for adults, our dogs also need to be safely confined inside a moving vehicle. There is a variety of products for canine car comfort available in pet supply stores and catalogs. Depending on the size of your dog and your vehicle, you might consider crates or canine seatbelts to prevent canine free reign. Station wagons can be fitted with grates that keep your passenger in the back compartment.

Chipper rides in the back seat with her 60-pound-plus body safe in a canine hammock. The canvas sling hangs over the backseat and clips around the front and back headrests. It limits the movement of large dogs and saves wear and tear on the upholstery. Small breeds can sit in a canine booster seat that snaps into place with the seat belts or in a cozy pet carrier that can also be attached with a seat belt. If you want to let your dog stick his head out the window after he is fastened in, think about fitting him with protective plastic goggles specially designed for dogs. This way, he can hang out the window without the risk of a bug or bit of debris lodging in his eyes.

A final safety tip: Always put your dog's leash on before you open the door to prevent him from bolting out and getting hurt in traffic or lost. This is the ideal setting to reinforce the *wait* cue.

On the Road with Rover

Q My husband and I are retired and we have always wanted to trek cross-country by car. Next summer there's a family reunion in Maine, so we plan to drive there from our home in Oregon. We want to take the time to enjoy this country from coast to coast, and we want to take our fox terrier with us. Sammy loves to ride in the car and is well behaved. Do you have any advice for finding pet-friendly hotels and tips for traveling with dogs?

A Like you, more and more travelers are taking their dogs on vacation these days. Fortunately, there is an increasingly wide range of lodgings, from the inexpensive to the luxurious, that are putting out the welcome mat for doggy guests. Over the past few years, my dogs and I have stayed in bargain-priced motels and oh-so-canine-fine hotels with doggy spas. Some places offer dog-walking services and doggy day care. At one fancy resort, Chipper was treated to a three-hour guided hike, followed by a pet massage and bath, and she loved the attention!

The fact that you are not in a hurry, and that Sammy is a seasoned, well-mannered traveler, can make your trip truly memorable. My first piece of advice is to heed the Golden Rule of Traveling: never try to sneak your dog into a hotel that doesn't permit pets. You risk losing a night's charge as a penalty and after a full day of driving, you may find yourselves unable to find a more accommodating option nearby.

If you belong to AAA or another motorist organization, stop by their local office for a book listing pet-friendly hotels. There are also several Web sites that identify lodgings that accept canine guests (see Resources, page 314). Chat with your friends who travel with their dogs and ask them for recommendations. When booking, ask the hotel if they have special pet rooms and what the pet deposit fee is. Some are refundable, but some are not. If possible, request a room on the first floor away from the high-traffic areas. Find out where you can take Sammy for his bathroom needs and what the cleanup requirements are.

Take along a small sign to hang on the doorknob to alert the housekeeping staff that Sammy is inside. Some places provide customized privacy signs that notify visitors that one of the guests inside has four legs, but have your own just in case. (See Travel Tips for Rover on page 257 for a list of other important items to pack.)

No matter how well behaved he is at home,

PAW PRINTS

Sigmund Freud believed that dogs possess a special sense for human emotions. His chow, Jo-Fi, assisted the great psychoanalyst in his sessions by alerting him to patients' moods. The dog would stay across the room from patients who were stressed or tense. Freud also realized that petting a dog could help calm and relax people.

do not let Sammy have free reign inside the room unsupervised. When you and your husband go to dinner or check out a tourist attraction, leave him in a crate after his exercise with all his creature comforts (water, favorite chew toy, and bedding) and tune the television or radio on low to muffle hallway sounds. Never leave him in a crate for more than a few hours. Another option is to bring a portable gate that keeps him safely in the bathroom area and set up a cozy spot for him there.

When you take Sammy out of your room, he needs to be on his best behavior. When you are at the front desk, put him in a *sit-stay*. That simple obedience cue wows the staff and generates positive comments from other guests. A dog who is friendly and well behaved will usually become a favorite with staff and guests alike, especially if he performs a couple of cool tricks as well.

Finally, always tidy up as you prepare to check out and leave the housekeeping staff a nice tip. These gestures create a positive impression that will benefit other pet lovers desiring to travel with their canine chums.

TRAVEL TIPS FOR ROVER

If you frequently take your dog with you in the car, keep a kit with doggy travel essentials in your trunk. My must-have list includes a water bowl, bottled water, extra leash and collar with identification tags, poop bags, an old towel, pre-moistened wipes, a basic first-aid kit, necessary medications, a copy of health records, bedding, treats, and at least a one-day supply of food.

During your trip, watch for any signs of motion sickness, dehydration, or other health issues. On a long drive, stop every couple of hours to let your dog stretch, have a drink, relieve himself, and move around for a few minutes.

Most important, pay attention to the weather. You've heard it before, but the facts are frightening: Dogs left inside cars during the summer can suffer from heat exhaustion and die within minutes, even with the windows open. When you are driving, turn on the air conditioner when temperatures start to sizzle and make sure the vents are directing cool air to the back seat.

Bear and Cubby Behave

BILL AND BETTY'S OLD ENGLISH SHEEPDOGS were friendly with strangers, affectionate with their owners, and well behaved in public. At 18 months, however, Cubby, an intact male, began challenging his five-year-old companion. He bullied Bear so much that the older dog retaliated. The two fought over toys, food bowls, personal space, and time with the couple. When the couple played with Cubby in the backyard, Bear would stand back and bark loudly. Inside the house, the dogs rushed to be the first through doorways and jostled for position at feeding time. Ugly spats occurred daily, and both humans were injured attempting to break up fights.

My analysis was that Cubby was competing with Bear for priority access to valued resources. Bear, not wanting to relinquish his position, fought back. Younger dogs may act pushy when they see an opportunity provided by the owner, which gives them enough confidence to try to take over. They act out because they don't see a clear line of command and feel they must step in. In this case, Betty was unwittingly causing a problem by giving the younger dog more attention.

To stop this sibling rivalry, I instructed Bill and Betty to elevate their leadership over both dogs to clearly communicate that *they* were the leaders in the household pack. Dogs need to know where they stand, even though there isn't always a strictly linear hierarchy. To reinforce the human role as top dog, so to speak, Bill and Betty instituted the "Please, Mother may I?" mode. Bear and Cubby were required to *sit, down,* and *stay* before receiving food, walks, toys, and attention. A focus on rewarding good behavior rather than punishing mistakes helped the dogs learn more acceptable behavior.

As it was Cubby who was starting the fights, Bill and Betty needed to reinforce Bear's status as the senior dog. Bear was fed first, exercised first, and allowed to walk ahead of Cubby. When approaching a doorway, both dogs had to sit politely before being allowed to proceed in order.

During the transition, I emphasized taking precautionary steps to avoid confrontations between the two dogs whenever possible and advised the couple to pick up all toys and to feed the dogs separately. The couple enrolled both dogs in a basic obedience class, which enhanced Bill and Betty's authority. Both dogs received 20 to 30 minutes of supervised aerobic activity each day to increase serotonin levels and promote a sense of calmness.

Within four months, the number of feuds dropped to fewer than once a week. After six months, the two dogs seemed to understand their rankings, and the fighting stopped. Cubby was gracious about his demotion and Bear was relaxed as top dog.

Contributed by Alice Moon-Fanelli, PhD

Table for Two, Please

Q When the weather is nice, a lot of cafés in my town have outdoor seating, and they allow dogs if they are on leashes and behave nicely. My dog, Madison, listens to me, but I often observe rude behavior by other dogs who are out of control. What can I do to avoid people whose dogs shouldn't be allowed in public?

A You have unleashed a topic that brings out the barker in me. Outdoor eateries offer dogs the chance to show off good manners and to hang out with you, instead of being stuck at home. Unfortunately, the percentage of eateries that permit dogs is shrinking because of the failure of dog owners to exercise some basic dining etiquette. Food managers don't want dogs who yap, wrestle, or roam freely from table to table — it's bad for business.

In my hometown, there are three outdoor eateries that allow dogs at our beautiful harbor area. Chipper is welcome at all three places because she practically becomes invisible once we are shown to our table. She sits or lies down and remains quiet. No begging, no barking. Often, diners at nearby tables have no clue until we stand up to leave that a 60-pound dog was just a handshake away.

You can't control your environment entirely, but you can take steps to heighten the chance of enjoying a pleasant outing with Madison in tow. Here are some tips for a delightful dining experience.

- ◆ **TRY TO DINE** during off-peak times, such as mid-morning and late afternoon. Weekdays are usually quieter than weekends.

- ◆ **PICK A SIX-FOOT OR FOUR-FOOT LEASH** that you can securely tether around one of your chair legs to keep your dog from roaming freely or disturbing other diners. If your dog is particularly active, accustom him to wearing a head halter in addition to being tethered in place.

- ◆ **REQUEST A TABLE** in an out-of-the-way corner. Dogs like to have a view in front of them and a wall behind them to keep people from sneaking up on them.

- ◆ **RESIST THE TEMPTATION** to have Madison meet and greet other dining dogs. Introductions should be saved for after mealtime and should take place in a spacious, public place. Politely let intrusive owners know of your wishes.

- ◆ **ALWAYS TAKE MADISON** on a vigorous power walk or play a game of fetch before you head for the eatery. This allows her to have a bathroom break and work off some energy so she is ready to rest when you're ready to order. Don't test her patience by staying so long that she becomes restless.

- **SCOPE OUT THE EATERY** before you step inside. Look for other dogs and see how they are behaving and how their owners are reacting to them. Steer clear if you see an owner desperately yanking on a leash or allowing his dog to bark at passersby or to bully another dog.

- **POLITELY REQUEST A WATER BOWL** for your dog (with ice, if she prefers it that way!).

- **LEAVE A GENEROUS TIP** — the waiter will remember and be more apt to accommodate you and Madison on your next visit.

Fashions for Fido

Q Whenever I go to my local pet supply store, I see all kinds of dog sweaters, hats, and other outfits for sale. I'm tempted to buy something, because I love to shop for clothes and I know my darling Yorkie, Minette, would look absolutely adorable in some of these outfits. But I'm not sure she would enjoy wearing clothes. How can I tell if she minds if I dress her up in some clothing designed for canines?

A Dog clothing has become a huge category in the pet products market, and manufacturers are producing all kinds of canine garb these days. You can buy scarves, booties, jackets, bathing suits, and even bridal gowns and tuxedos for dogs. Owners of toy breeds like the Pomeranian, Yorkshire terrier and toy poodle especially seem to like dressing their dogs in some of this clothing. It's almost as if they are reliving their childhood days of dolls and accessories.

To find out how your dog feels about wearing this kind of stuff, first think about her personality. Is Minette a happy-go-lucky dog who likes different experiences and eagerly greets new people? Or is she shy and withdrawn? Does she enjoy being handled and held, or does she just tolerate physical attention? Confident, happy dogs are much more likely to accept clothing than are dogs who are easily frightened by strange objects and new things.

If Minette seems like a good candidate for apparel, your next step is to buy a single outfit. Don't get carried away until you're sure she wants a new wardrobe! Make sure you get the right size so the clothes fit properly. Most dog apparel packaging provides guidelines on how to determine the correct size for your dog. The label may indicate the size based on the dog's weight or breed.

Before you dress Minette up in her outfit, give her some treats to let her know that something fun is about to happen. When she's focused on you and in a happy state of mind, take the clothing out of the packaging and show it to her. Let her sniff it while you talk to her in a happy voice. Make sure she isn't afraid of the clothing before you go to the next step. By the way, have your first fitting at home, where Minette feels safe and comfortable.

When Minette ignores the clothing and focuses on you and the treats you've been giving her, it's time for the fashion show. Gently and slowly place the clothes on the dog as you reassure her. Make sure Minette is comfortable with the process. If she becomes frightened, stop what you are doing and give her more treats.

Once she is dressed, let her walk around to get used to the new sensation. Praise her and talk in an enthusiastic voice to let her know that wearing clothes is a good thing. At first, she may seem awkward and confused, but after a few minutes, you should be able to get a sense as to whether Minette minds the apparel. If she is happy, with her tail up and a pleased look on her face, then you know she doesn't have a problem with wearing canine garb. If she starts strutting her stuff, congratulations! You definitely own a diva dog who is delighted to don the latest in canine fashions.

If she walks around with tail drooping, head low, and ears down, however, you have an unhappy dog on your hands. If she bites at or tries to paw off the clothing, then she is definitely conveying her displeasure in being dolled up. If this is the case, try to adjust her attitude by talking to her in a happy voice and offering her plenty of treats. If she continues to mope, or starts to act this way whenever she knows you are about to dress her up, you'll know that Minette prefers to wear only the fur she was born with.

Cough! Cough! Secondhand Smoke Dangers

Q I hope you can settle an argument in my family. My husband smokes about a pack of cigarettes a day. He usually smokes outside, but sometimes he smokes in the living room or bedroom. I know the dangers of secondhand smoke for nonsmoking people, but aren't our dogs, Bella and Belagio, also at risk? What information can I share with him to convince him to stop smoking, or at least to smoke outside, away from me and the dogs?

A You are right that cigarette smoking negatively affects the health of household pets. Tobacco smoke contains more than 4,000 chemicals of which nearly 50, including nicotine, are known carcinogens. Chemicals from cigarette smoke can land on a pet's hair and enter the body through the nostrils. When a dog or cat grooms himself, these chemicals are ingested, putting them at heightened risk for developing respiratory infections, asthma, and other conditions. A recent study conducted by researchers at Cummings School of Veterinary Medicine at Tufts University, published in the *American Journal of Epidemiology,* found that the risk of developing lymphoma tripled for cats and dogs exposed to secondhand tobacco smoke for five years or more. For pets living in households with two or more smokers, the risk for this type of cancer increased by a factor of four.

The bottom line: Actively support your husband in kicking his smoking habit and you'll improve the health of all members of your household, including your two dogs. Quitting smoking is very difficult, but if your husband won't quit for his own health, knowing the effects secondhand smoke has on your beloved dogs might make a difference.

A friend of mine smoked nearly a pack of cigarettes a day for 20 years, but she never found the motivation to stop. The Tufts findings were enough to convince her to stop smoking to protect the health of her five cats. As she told me, "People can decide if and when they're going to smoke, but their four-legged friends can't."

> **BREED BYTE**
>
> **If you have a basset hound, keep him on dry land. With two-thirds of their weight up front and those short, stubby legs, bassets are not good swimmers, so don't expect to see them doing laps with the Labradors.**

Ahh, There's the Rub!

Q I attended a pet expo where one of the booths featured a dog-massage therapist. At first I laughed, but then I watched closely and noticed that the dogs seemed to really enjoy having massages. They all lay there quietly looking relaxed; one even fell asleep! Are massages good for dogs, and should I consider giving Dolly, my Dalmatian, massages at home?

A Therapeutic massage knows no boundaries, even of species. The purposeful kneading and pressing and the circular motion help loosen muscle knots, unleash tension, and increase blood flow and range of motion in all sorts of creatures. Regular massages can work wonders for a dog's muscles and for her temperament as well. A nice massage not only warms body tissues and removes toxins and wastes from the body, but also conditions your dog to being touched, improves socialization, and bolsters your friendship bond. Dalmatians tend to be a bit energetic, so regular massage sessions might instill some calmness and relaxation in Dolly.

Once you learn massage, I guarantee that you will never pet your dog the same way again — no more head pats or back thumps. Here are some tips from Sue Furman, associate professor of anatomy and neurobiology at Colorado State University and one of the country's top canine- and equine-massage therapy instructors.

- ◆ **SELECT THE RIGHT TIME** to do a doggy massage — after a long walk or when Dolly has just woken up and is still sleepy and relaxed. She should welcome the massage, not resist it.

- ◆ **PICK A QUIET PLACE** free of distractions and temptations so Dolly can focus on your healing hands and fully enjoy the experience.

- ◆ **NEVER USE MASSAGE OILS.** Clean your hands before you begin.

- ◆ **USE YOUR HANDS AND FINGERTIPS,** not your nails, to make slow, deliberate movements. An easy position is the open hand. With your palm facing down, apply

gentle pressure in long, flowing strokes from Dolly's head to tail. Another easy stroke is called "finger circles." Use the tips of your fingers and make small, tight circles on your dog's muscles in clockwise and counterclockwise directions.

♦ **PAY ATTENTION** to Dolly's feedback signs. Continue if she is relaxed and stop when she becomes restless.

> **SNIFF IT OUT**
> Several scientific studies have shown that owning a pet may reduce blood pressure and lower cholesterol. Pets also seem to help people cope better with stress, loneliness, and depression.

♦ **LOOK FOR ANY SUSPICIOUS LUMPS** or bumps or signs of fleas or ticks during your massage session. Be on the alert for any stiff or sore muscles.

Check with local veterinary clinics or animal shelters to find out where canine massage classes are being held. I promise it will be one of the most fun and beneficial classes you've ever attended. But Dolly shouldn't be the only one in your household getting massages. Book a monthly appointment with a massage therapist and treat yourself as well!

GET FIT WITH FIDO

Say the word exercise and many people respond with one word: *ugh.* Or they come up with excuses for not making it to the gym or breaking out their bike. But the secret to improved health is just a tail wag away. Who needs expensive home equipment or a gym membership when you have a canine workout buddy?

Dan Hamner, a sports medicine doctor from New York City and proud owner of a small but fit dog, often tells his patients to replace the word *exercise* with *motion.* A national study by the American Heart Association reported that burning 2,000 calories a week by performing a physical activity — such as walking an hour every day — could increase life expectancy by two full years.

Maintaining a regular fitness program with your dog delivers many dividends for both of you: improved health; greater flexibility and strength; reduced risk for arthritis, diabetes, and heart disease; and my favorite, spending less money on veterinary and doctor bills.

Before you lace your sneakers and grab the leash to go on a power walk, book appointments for both of you for physical examinations. Discuss workout options that are best for you and your dog. Keep in mind that an activity that may work for one dog, may not work for another. Dogs with flat faces, such as bulldogs, do not tolerate the heat easily. Long-legged dogs such as greyhounds can cover distance more effortlessly than, say, a short-legged basset hound.

Spend a few minutes warming up and helping your dog prepare his muscles, too. Have him sit up and beg, then play bow, roll over, and slowly walk in a large circle. Start modestly with a five-minute walk. Strive to increase the distance and pace to 30 minutes or longer. For longer walks, bring a water bottle for you and a collapsible bowl for your pal.

Other workout options include swimming and hiking. You might even try a more dog-focused activity like agility or canine musical freestyle. (See Canine Jocks Rule, page 202 for more suggestions.)

Turn Ho-Hum into Hooray!

Q I know it is important to walk my dog every day, but it is boring. I sense that Tippy, my corgi, is bored, too. We walk around our neighborhood for about 20 minutes twice a day. Tippy smells the same mailboxes, the same grass, the same car tires. I know that dogs like routines, but what can we do to break the monotony and make walks more interesting and fun?

A Dogs live by the motto "So Many Smells, So Little Time." In Tippy's case, he surely can tell you every single thing that is within your 20-minute range, so it's time for new frontiers. Start by varying your routes, the duration of your walks, and, if possible, the time of day that you walk. Simply switching to the other side of the street will introduce Tippy to a bonanza of new sights, sounds, and smells. Invite a friend with a friendly dog who likes Tippy to join you on your walks. Having company will liven up the routine for both of you. If your weekday walks must follow your work schedule, take time on the weekends to drive Tippy to a pet-friendly place for a longer hike. Or, treat him to playtime at a local dog park if he likes to play with other dogs.

Daily walks provide golden opportunities for you to reinforce basic obedience training and introduce new tricks. Unleash some fun, creative ways to bust boredom on your regular treks with my four favorite walking games: the Molasses Walk, the Jackrabbit Sprint, Park It Here, and Curbside Attraction. Your increased activity may evoke some giggles and stares from onlookers, so bring your sense of humor with you on the walks. Act goofy and it will be contagious to Tippy and others.

The Molasses Walk begins with Tippy walking nicely at your side with the leash loose. Ask Tippy to look at you as you take giant steps forward in slow motion saying *s-l-o-w* in a drawn-out way. The goal is for Tippy to copy your slow stride. When he does, reward him with praise *(good slow!)* and a treat. Continue doing this slow walk for 10 or 15 seconds and then return to a normal pace.

Next, hasten the pace with the Jackrabbit Sprint. Start power walking and in an exuberant tone tell Tippy to go *fast, fast, fast, fast!* (Be careful not to move so quickly that you are dragging him behind you, though!) Keep this pace up for 10 or 15 seconds and then stop. Give him a treat and resume your normal walk.

In addition to varying the pace, spice up your walks with my Park It Here game. Depending on the size of your dog and his physical condition, pick a park bench or sturdy low surface onto which he can easily jump. Train Tippy by tapping your hand on the bench, then making a sweeping up motion as you say *jump up!* Help him initially by hoisting him up if he seems confused by this strange request. Once he is on the bench, make him sit for a few seconds before giving him permission to leap off. Praise and treat and be on the lookout for the next bench for Tippy to conquer.

The Curbside Attraction trick makes crossing the street more interesting. Stand on a quiet street (very close to the curb, so you don't risk getting hit by a car). Face Tippy. Ask him to sit, and then use a treat to slowly lure him forward — the idea is have him move just his front feet. As soon as his front legs touch the street and his back legs remain on the curb, reinforce the pose by saying *curb*. At the same time, put your open hand in front of his face to stop him from continuing to move forward into the street. Praise and treat. This looks quite comical, but dogs have senses of humor, too.

These are just a few suggestions for spicing up your walks. If you vary your routine and make up your own fun games, I'm sure both you and Tippy will enjoy your daily outings more.

DON'T OVERDO IT

Be careful not to overexert your dog on walks and during activities. If your dog keeps up with you on a walk or tends to pull out ahead, but is now walking beside you, or even lagging a bit behind you, he may be asking to rest. If he displays any of the following signs, stop the activity and allow him to rest.

Drooping tongue

Rapid panting — an early sign of overheating

Hesitation — taking a few extra seconds before retrieving a tossed ball

Weight shifting — using different muscle groups to offset soreness

Staggering

Muscle tremors

Limping — check footpads for cuts and bruises and legs for sprains or muscle pulls

TEMPORARY DOGS

Owning a dog is typically a lifetime arrangement. However, if you have room in your heart and your home for a temporary dog, you might consider offering short-term care for a needy canine. Many animal shelters and rescue organizations are desperate for foster homes for dogs needing extra attention.

Another way to help dogs and people in transition is to act as a foster home for the pets of women who are victims of domestic violence. Ask at a social services agency, shelter for women, or humane society to see if there is such a program in your area.

If you have lots of time and patience, think about becoming a puppy trainer for a service dog organization. These programs take a serious commitment and an understanding that you are just "starting" the puppy for someone else. There are several national programs where you can find more information — see Resources, page 315, for details.

PART VI

Changing Lives, Parting Ways

In my days as a daily newspaper reporter, I marveled at how my favorite metro editor could juggle so many things so well. She seemed to take the hiring and firing of staff members and the changes in layout and design in stride. She shared her secret to survival: recognizing that the only constant in life was change. That adage certainly holds true when it comes to our dogs. Many of us adopt puppies or young adult dogs with the good intention of keeping them for the rest of their lives.

Sadly, life can interfere with our best intentions. Events like divorce, the birth of a baby, relocating, or the onset of pet allergies change our ability to provide a home for our pets. Sometimes behavior issues arise that seem impossible to cure. If our dogs do spend their whole lives with us, we must face that time we wish never would occur: parting ways with our canine friend because of his death or our own.

We can't stop change and we can't live forever. But we do our best to prepare for the unexpected curveballs life hurls our way, such as divorce and death and other changes in our lives.

Doggy Dementia

Q Zeke, my black-and-tan terrier mix, is 15. She used to love stalking squirrels, but now she would rather sleep all day. On walks, she can be only a few feet away from me but all of a sudden will start looking all around and acting as if she has completely lost me. In the house, she sometimes stares blankly at the walls. Can dogs develop dementia in the way people do?

A I am sorry to hear about Zeke. Memory loss and signs of confusion in older dogs may be symptoms of cognitive dysfunction syndrome, which is often described with the acronym DISH, for disorientation, interaction reduction, sleep difficulties, and house soiling. Zeke is clearly disoriented, because she wanders aimlessly, becomes lost in your house, and stares blankly at walls. You may have noticed other changes in her behavior as well. Sleeping more during the day, waking up in the middle of the night, and barking for no apparent reason are also telltale signs. House soiling by a senior dog can be caused by forgetfulness but may be a sign of a medical problem.

In the past, owners — as well as many veterinarians — usually dismissed these symptoms as normal signs of aging. But today, growing gray in the muzzle doesn't have to automatically mean cognitive dysfunction. I encourage you to take Zeke for a thorough veterinary exam. As they age, dogs need more frequent checkups, and many veterinarians recommend a senior wellness exam. This particular series of tests at age seven (sooner for giant breeds) establishes a baseline of health and can uncover potentially serious problems before symptoms become unmanageable. Fortunately, treatments are now available that may not cure age-related canine dysfunction but can at least slow down the degenerative process.

In addition to a visit to your family veterinarian, you might consider consulting a veterinary specialist who can perform specific tests, such as ultrasound or MRI, to determine if there is a medical reason (age-related kidney or liver problems, for example) for changes in Zeke's behavior or if Zeke is displaying signs of cognitive dysfunction syndrome.

You can't put the brakes on the number of birthdays your dog accumulates, but you can take purposeful steps to keep her feeling years younger. Veterinary researchers are learning ways to manage canine senility with memory-improving medications and specially formulated senior dog foods to ensure that a dog's final years are happy and healthy. There are several ways you can make Zeke's final years truly golden.

◆ **KEEP YOUR DOG MENTALLY STIMULATED** by playing a game of hide-and-seek with food treats stashed in different rooms of the house. Or serve up interesting food puzzles, such as a peanut butter–filled, hard rubber hollow toy.

- ◆ **MAKE A LIST OF ALL THE SYMPTOMS** you have noticed before visiting your veterinarian, including, for example, if your dog seems to forget her name, fails to greet you when you come home, or wanders away from you in the middle of receiving affection. Also report any changes in appetite, elimination habits, and physical condition.

- ◆ **REINFORCE BASIC COMMANDS** and add some new ones. You *can* teach an old dog new tricks, and doing so helps keep her mind alert and functioning. Teach her to sit before you head out the door for a walk or to shake paws before you set down her food bowl. (If her hearing is fading, you can teach her to look to you for hand signals.)

- ◆ **TAKE SHORTER BUT MORE FREQUENT WALKS,** if possible. Regular exercise increases oxygen delivery to the brain, which can help your dog's mental abilities and keep her aging muscles working more smoothly. Stick to smooth surfaces that won't jar her joints. Vary the routes to stimulate her senses by exposing her to new sights, sounds, and smells.

- ◆ **ENCOURAGE YOUR DOG TO STRETCH.** Prior to playtime or walks, have your dog get into a play bow position — head down, front legs low and stretched forward, and back end up. Lure your dog into this fun posture by lowering a treat under her nose. This natural full-body stretch helps improve circulation and warm the muscles. After a walk or activity, gently stretch your dog's legs and massage her torso.

◆ **PROVIDE PLENTY OF WATER.** As dogs age, they tend to drink less and run the risk of dehydration. Add a few more water bowls around your home and measure the water in the morning and at night to make sure your dog drinks enough water. Wipe up spills so that she doesn't slip and injure herself.

Unfortunately, our dogs don't live forever, but these measures can make Zeke's senior days better ones for the both of you.

Time to Retire?

Q About three times a week, I take Nugget, my certified therapy dog, on visits to a nursing home and a children's cancer hospital. We spend an hour or two greeting the residents. Nugget has been a therapy dog for about eight years and at age ten, she's a senior herself! Lately, I've noticed that she isn't as excited as she used to be when I put on her therapy vest, and she takes forever to get into the car. When she comes home from a therapy visit, she seems to be sad and a bit down. Why is she acting this way?

A I regard therapy dogs as the canine versions of Bob Hope when he did his USO tours to troops. Nugget also has brought smiles and happiness to many nursing home residents and sick children who are lonely and away from home. Although Labrador retrievers rank at the top in terms of the number of certified therapy dogs, dogs of any breed can do this work if they have the right temperament and enjoy being around all types of people. Therapy dogs need a thorough grounding in obedience training; they must be able to sit patiently by a wheelchair or hospital bed, to withstand a lot of noise and distractions without fear, and to tolerate having their ears pulled and their tails yanked by people without reacting aggressively. Many learn to gently place a paw on a lap or to nudge a patient's hand to encourage interaction.

Animal-assisted programs can change and even save lives. It is just as important, however, that the therapy dogs' needs are met, too. Owners need to be on the lookout for signs of stress or burnout in their four-legged ambassadors of love. Therapy dogs are emotionally affected by sadness and pain in those they visit. They can get stressed and exhausted. It takes two to make a good therapy team, and both must be committed to performing the task. It sounds as though you and Nugget have done a lot of good together, but even though you may still love the visits, you need to respect Nugget's wishes. She is showing signs that she is ready for retirement.

Therapy dogs who are ready to go home, or retire completely, will respond more slowly to cues. They will become more distracted on visits and may spend more time at the water bowl than working with the patients. Sometimes a dog will want to spend more time visiting one resident at the hospital instead of making the rounds.

Nugget, in her own sweet way, is letting you know that after eight years of service, she is ready to spend more time in your home than in a nursing home or hospital. You need to honor her message. In some cases, retired therapy dogs happily take on a new role of serving as a temperament test dog for other dogs being tested for therapy work. Perhaps Nugget can usher in a new generation of therapy dogs in your city.

Tips for Golden Oldies

Q The other day I was caught off guard when I took a close look at my dog, Benji, and realized how gray his muzzle has become. It seems like just yesterday that he was a rambunctious puppy, but he is nearly 10. He pauses now before he gingerly jumps up on the sofa or on my bed, and it takes him a while to loosen up in the mornings when we go on our walks. Are there any ways I can pamper him without spending a lot of money? I am a senior myself and on a fixed income.

A The graying of America has begun and that applies to both people and dogs. One out of every three dogs — about 18 million — is seven years or older. For most breeds, that equates to senior citizenship status. We get AARP cards at age 50; perhaps dogs should get AARF cards when they reach the equivalent milestone birthday!

Since Benji has been your faithful pal since his puppy days, he deserves a bit of pampering. One thing you should spend some money on is a checkup at the veterinary clinic. Two common reasons for aging dogs to require extra coaxing to get on or off furniture or in and out of cars are arthritis and hip dysplasia. You also should rule out an acute injury. Please book a senior wellness appointment for Benji to identify the reason behind his stiffness. The bigger the dog (and the more overweight), the greater the risk for hip problems, especially in the senior years. There is no cure for hip dysplasia or arthritis, but medication, weight control, and gentle exercise can minimize Benji's pain and maximize his mobility.

Here are some other suggestions that won't take a bite out of your wallet. Treat Benji to regular therapeutic massages. Just five to ten minutes a day can help maintain his muscle tone, range of motion in the joints, and comfort level. Practice a technique called "effleurage," French for light massage. It is petting with a purpose. Have Benji sit, stand, or lie down on his belly. Start by putting one hand on his shoulder or side to comfort him and use the other to pet him front to back with your palm. You can use more pressure if Benji is not in pain, but for a dog with severe joint problems, gently stroke from the knee up to the hip and the mid-back to move that extra fluid out and reduce swelling.

You can also temporarily improve circulation in Benji's hips by warming a damp, not wet, towel in the dryer for 10 to 15 minutes and placing it on his hips while he's resting. The moisture in the towel retains heat better. This pampering works wonders on dogs of all ages. Don't use an electric heating pad on a dog because he might chew the cord. You may also risk setting the temperature too high and burning him.

Take a sturdy box or plastic milk crate and place it upside down next to your bed or sofa to create a step for Benji to hoist himself up and down more easily. If you are handy with tools, you can create an inexpensive ramp using old carpet remnants or rugs and blocks of wood.

Pay attention to any signs of fading eyesight or hearing. Be sure to give him more frequent bathroom breaks and keep tabs on the health of his teeth and gums in case he needs to switch to softer food. With loving care, I'm sure Benji will enjoy his last years in comfort.

A DOG'S AGE IN HUMAN YEARS

The old saying that one year in a dog's life equals seven human years is roughly true, but the following chart gives a more accurate comparison based on the dog's weight.

Age of dog	0–20 lbs	21–50 lbs	51–90 lbs	>90 lbs
5	36	37	40	42
6	40	42	45	49
7	44	47	50	56
8	48	51	55	64
9	52	56	61	71
10	56	60	66	78
11	60	65	72	86
12	64	69	77	93
13	68	74	82	101
14	72	78	88	108
15	76	83	93	115
16	80	87	99	123
17	84	92	104	
18	88	96	109	
19	92	101	115	

■ = adult   ■ = senior   ■ = geriatric

Created by Dr. Fred Metzner, DVM, State College, PA

Casey and Tasha's Happy Golden Years

I FIRST MET RHONDA when she came to me for private lessons for Casey, her young golden retriever. Casey was not an easy dog to train and he exhibited aggressive behavior around his food bowl and bones. But with the use of positive reinforcement and the discovery that part of his behavior was due to treatable hypothyroidism, he blossomed into a wonderful sweet dog. About four years later, Rhonda got a second golden retriever puppy, an exuberant sociable girl she named Tasha. They did well in my puppy classes and advanced training classes.

Then Rhonda's elderly parents, Frank and Dottie, came to live with her. Dottie had Parkinson's disease and used a walker. Rhonda's biggest fear was that her big dogs would unintentionally knock over her parents and injure them.

I recommended that we train Casey and Tasha to be useful in Dottie's physical therapy. Casey learned to lay his head in Dottie's lap so she could exercise her hands by petting him. She also brushed both dogs and tossed balls for them to retrieve.

I worked with Rhonda in teaching both verbal commands and hand signals to the dogs because Parkinson's disease can sometimes make it difficult to speak. Casey and Tasha learned to wait for the release word or hand signal to move. This enabled Frank and Dottie to walk through the house without the fear of being knocked over.

The added training and responsibility of Casey and Tasha gave Dottie a sense of purpose. The dogs were her constant companions. She knew she had an incurable disease that would get worse with time, but keeping her mobile helped to extend her quality of life. Had it not been for the dogs and their training, her condition could have deteriorated to the point where she would have needed to move to a nursing home. She was able to take care of her basic needs up until she died.

Frank became depressed after Dottie's death, but we convinced him to take Tasha to my training classes. He wasn't keen on the idea at first but said he would give it a try for Tasha's sake. After a few weeks, Frank began to look forward to going to class with Tasha. He would spend time each day at home doing his homework assignment, being certain to pass on what he learned in class to Casey, too. Frank and Tasha excelled, completing five levels of training before Frank died at age 86.

I share this story because, without training, Casey and Tasha could have caused injury to Rhonda's parents. Instead, the dogs helped Frank and Dottie enjoy their final years.

Contributed by Pia Silvani, CPDT

How Pets Express Grief

Q Our two dogs, Bosco and Bubba, and our cat, Clyde, were inseparable buddies. We often remarked how lucky we were never to have to deal with jealousy issues among our loving trio. Bubba, our fun-loving bullmastiff, recently became very ill, and we asked our veterinarian to come to the house to euthanize him. We did this in the presence of Bosco and Clyde. Now both of them seem so sad all the time. They eat a little, but don't beg for food, and Bosco is usually a chow-hound. Are dogs and cats capable of grieving the loss of another pet?

A Not all pets suffer grief at the loss of another pet in the household, but your trio forged a strong and loving friendship, and the two that remain are definitely feeling the loss of their companion. One sure sign of that is loss of appetite. Animals may show their distress by sitting around and moping, sleeping more, and not enjoying your company. Some may suddenly act aloof while others become clingy and needy.

You did a wonderful thing by including Bosco and Clyde in this farewell act for Bubba. Top veterinarians and animal behaviorists tell me that animals view death as a natural process like birth. Whenever possible, allow other household pets to sniff and inspect the body of the dead pet. Although there is no scientific evidence to support the notion that checking the body will help the surviving pets to cope emotionally, at least it lets them know for sure what has happened and, at best, may help bring closure.

When a pet dies away from home, out of sight and smell of the remaining pets in the household, the surviving pets may keep searching in vain for their pal. In a survey taken by the American Society for the Prevention of Cruelty to Animals (ASPCA), researchers found that 36 percent of dogs ate less than normal after a canine pal died. About 11 percent refused to eat at all, and 63 percent began to howl and vocalize more than normal. Overall, more than half — 66 percent — displayed four or more behavior changes after the death of a dog or cat companion.

To help Bosco and Clyde cope with the loss of Bubba, introduce them to new toys, entice them to play a favorite game, and offer high-value treats. Spend more time giving them affection and hugs. If their grief-related behaviors persist, please consult your veterinarian about temporarily giving them medication to cope with their depression or anxieties. Don't rush to bring home a new dog or cat, thinking that this newcomer will help ease their grief. Some people are so overcome by grief that they make mistakes during this "rebound" period and chose an inappropriate replacement pet. Introducing a new pet too soon may add to the sadness and confusion the survivors are feelings. Just as you do, Sammy and Clyde need time to properly grieve the loss of Bubba.

Knowing When to Say Good-bye

Q I love dogs but I hate that they don't live as long as we do. My latest dog, Sparky, has been diagnosed with bone cancer in his front leg. He is a feisty, friendly Chihuahua who is only seven years old. I know that even if we do beat this cancer, Sparky will eventually reach that point when he dies on his own or I must make that painful decision to put him to sleep. How will I know when it is the right time to euthanize him?

A Saying good-bye to a loyal pet is one of life's hardest decisions. If your dog becomes terminally ill or is critically injured, or the cost for treatment is financially beyond your means, euthanasia may be a valid option. Fortunately for Sparky, canine medicine has made amazing strides in treating cancer and other serious diseases. Cancer centers for companion animals now exist at veterinary schools as well as at privately funded research centers throughout the country. Bone cancer is serious, however, and it is wise to ask this question before it reaches the point where you don't have the time to carefully consider all options. The more you are able to prepare for the possible loss of your pet, the fewer regrets you will have.

Before Sparky becomes seriously ill, make an appointment with your veterinarian. Ask him or her to describe the methods and details of the euthanasia procedure. You may be amazed at how peaceful and pain-free this procedure is. Preparing for euthanasia includes determining when and where the procedure should take place. Your vet may be willing to make a house call. You will need to decide if you want your pet's body to be buried or cremated. Think about your own needs and decide whether you would prefer to be alone after the procedure or if you want to spend time with a special friend.

When is the right time? That is certainly an individual call, but quality of life is your guidepost in making the decision. You will probably know when it is right by paying careful attention to Sparky's signals. He may stop eating, be unable to go to the bathroom on his own, or begin to sleep all the time. Look for signs of pain or discomfort that cannot be eased with medication.

Please keep this final thought in mind: The very definition of euthanasia means a painless death to end physical suffering in our animal friends. It is truly the last gift we can give them.

BREED BYTE

Named for the region of Mexico where they were first bred in the mid-19th century, the Chihuahua stands short on stature but long on longevity. On average, this breed lives 18 to 20 years.

Inheriting a Pampered Pooch

Q My elderly grandmother died recently, leaving behind a four-year-old papillon named Sugar, who was a wonderful companion to her. My grandmother doted on this dog, serving her food on china plates, dressing her up with ribbons, and letting her sit in her own dining room chair. Grandma was also practical and discussed with me in advance how to care for Sugar after she died. I love Sugar, but it is clear that she misses my grandmother a lot. What can I do to help Sugar understand that she now has a new loving home?

A Your grandmother showed foresight in making sure that her sweet dog had a good home after she died. You will never behave the same way that she did with Sugar, but you can love her in your own fashion.

Our pets can't tell us in words how they feel when a beloved person leaves them, but they do display signs of mourning. Some dogs show amazing dedication to their deceased owners, so be aware that Sugar may show signs of stress and anxiety for some time as she adjusts to her new life with you. Sugar may urinate in your house when you're not around, not eat much, excessively lick her paws, or go overboard to greet you each time you come home. These behaviors can last days or weeks. Please consult your veterinarian concerning behavioral issues that affect your dog's health, especially lack of appetite.

Help Sugar adjust to your home by letting her sleep in your bedroom at night. Dogs are den creatures and this will give her some comfort and feeling of security. Offer her healthy outlets by walking her daily, engaging her in games like fetch, and keeping the television or radio on when you're not at home to provide some welcome human noise. Invite some dog-friendly guests over to dote on Sugar and improve her mood.

> **BREED BYTE**
> Papillon is the French word for "butterfly." This silky-coated toy breed is named for its large ears that look like butterfly wings.

You cannot replace your grandmother in the eyes of Sugar, but you do have a wonderful opportunity to form a new friendship with her and to provide her with a loving and stable home that honors your grandmother's memory.

> **PAW PRINTS**
> One of the best stories to illustrate the devotion of dogs is that of a terrier named Bobby whose owner died in Edinburgh, Scotland in the mid-1800s. Bobby attended the graveside service and then lay on his owner's grave every night for the next 14 years until his own death. Members of the town were so moved by this canine devotion that they erected a statue and water fountain in Bobby's memory that stands to this day.

How Do We Go On?

Q Our 10-year-old daughter Kelly has never known a day without Jelly, our tri-colored Australian shepherd, in her life. Jelly greeted Kelly with a friendly tail wag the day we brought her home from the hospital and kept a close eye on her throughout her toddler days, even keeping her away from the pool when she ventured too close. Sadly, Jelly developed a rapid form of cancer, and we made a family decision to euthanize her to spare her any more pain. We are all devastated by the loss of Jelly, especially Kelly. How can we help our daughter — and ourselves — cope?

A Over the past two decades, we have redefined our notion of family to include pets. For many couples, a dog or a cat often precedes the birth or adoption of a child. In essence, that pet becomes an older sibling to their child. Children who grow up with loving pets are fortunate to have wonderful memories that won't disappear. I still fondly remember my first dog, Nicky, even though I was just six when he died.

Grieving for a pet is distinct from other forms of mourning. There are no traditional ceremonies or social rituals for honoring a loyal dog or sweet cat. But a pet's presence punctuates our daily lives, and the loss can be keenly felt. Your family should feel free to grieve openly and embrace the special connection you had with Jelly. Recognize that you need to grieve before you can truly heal. Sudden crying spells, feelings of depression, and other swings of emotion are normal.

If parents don't show their sadness or grief, it sends a message to children that grief is wrong. Most psychologists and therapists agree that it is appropriate for parents to tell their children when they are feeling sad because they are missing their dog who died. Equally important is to tell your children that you love them and that you are open to talking about a deceased family pet.

According to Swiss psychiatrist Elisabeth Kubler-Ross, most people go through five steps of grief. These steps can apply to the loss of a family member or friend as well as a beloved pet. Here are the five stages.

DENIAL/SHOCK. "My dog is too young to die."

ANGER. "How dare my sweet dog be taken from me?"

BARGAINING. "Dear God, I will go to church more often if you bring my pet back to me."

DEPRESSION. "What's the point in eating or having fun anymore?"

ACCEPTANCE. "I miss my dog terribly, but I now know that he is no longer in pain."

Keep in mind it may take your children days, weeks, or even months to go through these stages. Recognize that not everyone experiences each of these steps or goes through them in a linear fashion. When grieving, be honest and avoid using euphemisms. Use the word *died* rather than *put to sleep,* particularly with children younger than 12. Otherwise, a child needing an operation in the future, for example, may hear the doctor say he'll be put to sleep for the procedure and become unduly frightened. In addition, avoid saying that God loved your dog so much that he brought him to heaven. Your child may wonder why God doesn't love him enough to bring him to heaven, too, or may become fearful that perhaps God does indeed love him enough to take him away.

Depending on a child's age and level of maturity, therapists offer these general guidelines to help parents discuss family pets' dying.

UNDER AGE 2. Babies and toddlers may sense the dog's death, based on feeling the stress and emotions expressed by other family members, but are unlikely to feel directly affected.

BETWEEN AGES 2 AND 5. Young children may be sad because they miss the family dog as a play pal. They have trouble realizing that death is permanent and may respond to the heightened stress in the family by thumb sucking, tantrums, and other problematic behaviors.

BETWEEN AGES 5 AND 9. Children start to recognize that death is permanent but may fantasize that death can be defied. At these ages, some children may harbor resentment for having to feed or care for the family dog and may secretly wish at times the dog would die. If the dog gets hit by a car and does die, these children may be filled with guilt. It's important for parents to let them know that accidents happen and they didn't cause the death.

AGES 10 AND OLDER. Children understand that living things eventually die, but some may have difficulty accepting that death is permanent. They may express anger or guilt at losing their pet, or become curious about death.

Here are some ways that you might help Kelly deal with her grief. Conduct a ceremony or memorial service at home. The greatest way to honor a dog's memory is to learn how you became a better person for having them in your life. Do this by acknowledging the ways in which your dog helped you grow and learn.

Spend some time with Kelly recalling happy, silly, fond memories of life with Jelly. Encourage her to write a letter or poem to and from Jelly. Putting words down on paper can sometimes ease grief. If you have time to think about this before the dog's death, you can purchase a kit that allows you to make clay impressions of your dog's paw print as a memento. Kelly could also make a special picture frame for a favorite photo.

Encourage Kelly to reach out to friends and other family members who can listen and recognize how sad she feels about Jelly's death. I also recommend calling a pet-loss hotline, available at most veterinary schools, or check with your local churches or veterinary clinics for pet-loss help referrals. Gently remind Kelly and yourself that Jelly isn't in pain any more. See Resources on page 315 for recommended readings that might help Kelly and other children deal with their sadness.

Exercising Will Power

Q I share my home with a cocker spaniel, a pug, and two cats. I hope to be around to provide for them to the end, but I know that I should have a plan in writing for how to care for them in case I die first. I would never want any of them to be abandoned, taken to an animal shelter, or be separated. They love each other. What kind of legal protection do I have to ensure that my wishes are carried out if I should die before my pets?

A You represent a growing number of pet owners who are drawing up wills, living trusts, and other legal documents that specify how their pets should be cared for — and by whom — in the event they become incapacitated or die before their pets do. Legally, pets are considered to be personal property, which means you have a right to determine what happens to them in the event of your death. You are absolutely right that any arrangements should be made in writing, because verbal agreements cannot be legally enforced.

Far too many beloved pets end up in shelters after their owners die unexpectedly or become ill and need to enter a nursing home. In the chaos, trauma, and upheaval that often occurs when someone dies, pets can easily be overlooked while funeral arrangements are being made. Prearranging the care of your pets gives you peace of mind, and it's never too early to make legal arrangements. The first step takes only a few minutes — and it's free. Here's what to do.

Keep a card in your wallet that specifies who should be contacted to take care of your pets in the event of an emergency. Include their phone numbers. Post this information on the front of your refrigerator or in another highly visible place in your home. Give a third copy to your veterinarian and to any pet caretakers, like doggy day care providers or kennel operators, and let family members know that you have made these plans. Make sure the people you are designating have agreed to be your pet's guardian!

Keep a separate file on each pet. Include the pet's medical history, a personality description, likes and dislikes, eating habits, how your pet relates to people and other animals, and most important, a labeled color photo. Provide a backup copy to your chosen caretaker. Separate files are important so there is no confusion about which pet needs which medication or special food.

Contact your county or state bar association for names of attorneys who practice estate planning and animal law. Be aware of the difference between wills and trusts.

Essentially, a will directs who gets what after a person dies. A trust can be implemented while you're still alive (should you no longer be able to care for your pet). Both can be changed or updated should you want to do so. There are many types of trusts, and they vary from state to state. With an honorary trust, for example, you can declare one person as trustee to be in charge of the money paid out for the care of your pets and another person in charge of the actual care of your pets. This can establish some important checks and balances.

If you do not have a friend or family member willing to care for your pets, look into pet retirement homes, sanctuaries, or shelters that set aside separate buildings that serve as long-term dog condos. Consult your veterinarian or animal behaviorist about a reputable shelter or animal organization you can designate to care for your pet. Ask for references and a written agreement that spells out your wishes. You can also name a shelter, veterinary hospital, or other animal agency as your beneficiary. In exchange for agreeing to be your pets' caretaker, you bequeath them your home or other asset.

Providing legal protection for pets is a growing area of the law. As much as we do not want to think about dying, it is important to determine who will take care of the pets we leave behind. These steps can ease your worries and provide a healthy, happy future for your pets.

Who Gets the Dog?

Q My husband and I are calling it quits after 10 years of marriage. We don't have children, but we do have a wonderful boxer named Ali who loves both of us. Ali was the runt of the litter, but at five years old, he is all muscle, sports a ready grin, and has brought us much joy. Our breakup has been fairly amicable, and we have agreed on who gets what, with the exception of Ali. We both want him. We are thinking about joint custody, but would that be best for Ali's emotional well-being?

A With the divorce rate at about 40 percent, more and more dogs are getting caught in an emotional tug-of-war between dueling spouses. When couples feud, the yelling, slamming doors, and icy silences can take an emotional and physical toll on their ever-loyal dogs. Just like kids, dogs can actually become physically ill because of the heightened level of stress in the house. Behavioral problems may develop, such as separation anxiety or signs of aggression.

Divorce often brings out the worst in people when emotions run high. Dogs can become pawns in divorce settlements, and they can become the real victims. I've heard of cases in which one spouse would not let the other spouse see the dog, and basically used the dog for leverage for a final settlement deal. But it doesn't have to be that way. Like you, many couples work out an amicable agreement

PAW PRINTS
At the end of the Beatles' song, *A Day in the Life*, Paul McCartney recorded an ultrasonic whistle, audible only to dogs, as a message for his Shetland sheepdog.

to share custody rather than using the dog as a weapon. To maintain a sense of normalcy for your dog, stick to your everyday routines as much as possible. Dogs are creatures of habit and look forward to regular activities, such as the Saturday trip to the dog park or their morning game of tug-of-war. They are adaptable, though, and can certainly adjust to different routines in two separate households.

Let me share the story of a couple who successfully kept their dog in mind during their divorce. This East Coast couple regarded their Labrador retriever as their four-legged kid and neither wanted to be without him. During their separation and ultimate divorce, Beau was the only topic the couple did not fight about. Neither wanted the dog to feel torn loyalties, so they worked out an informal custody arrangement in which Beau would switch households every six weeks to three months. The two now live about 250 miles apart, so they meet halfway to transfer Beau from one car to the other. Although he initially displayed confusion and sadness by barking and constantly seeking attention, Beau is always delighted to see the other person and has learned that he can be secure in two different places.

Sticking to familiar rituals is vital. When Beau is with the ex-husband, the two enjoy long daily walks. When

Beau stays with the ex-wife, they play a favorite game called "Shoe for a Chew." The rules are simple: Beau retrieves a shoe from the closet in exchange for a chew treat. During his absence, each owner occasionally sends Beau a small toy or treat with his or her scent on it, and they talk to him on the phone once in a while. Beau sniffs attentively when he receives a toy, card, or treat in the mail from one of his pet parents. Several years after the divorce, he happily moves between his households with no signs of stress or anxiety.

Banish the Packing Box Blues

Q With our kids out of college and starting their own lives, my wife and I find that our house in Connecticut is just too big for the two of us and Emma, our three-year-old spaniel. We have decided to take early retirement and move to a much smaller condo in one of our favorite vacation places, Palm Springs, CA. We are worried about Emma, who is very much a member of our family. She gets a bit nervous when there is a change in the daily routine. We don't know how she will react when she sees packing boxes all over the house and moving men coming through the front door. How can we make this move a smooth one for her?

A Congratulations on your plans to start over. Palm Springs is a very canine-friendly place with a dog park inside the city limits that is spacious, features well-mannered guests, and offers a spectacular view of the Santa Rosa Mountains.

Moving is one of life's big stressors for both dogs and people. The break in the routine with furniture being moved, items being packed, and strange men coming in and out of the house can take a toll on a dog's self-confidence and feeling of security. Fortunately, dogs tend to bond more with their people than zip codes. (Cats, by comparison, truly prefer to be homebodies.) The good news for Emma is that once she settles into the new locale, she will happily continue her great life with the two of you.

While you are in the process of packing your belongings and preparing the house for sale, maintain Emma's usual routine as much as possible, especially your daily walks — the exercise will help all of you unleash some tension and stress. Speak to her in an upbeat, happy voice to reassure her. Help her feel more comfortable with the changing household by setting up cardboard boxes in rooms all over your house. As you pack items, let Emma sniff and explore. Point out the box to her, say the word *box,* and then hand her a treat. You are building up a positive association between the boxes and the treats for Emma. Take a break once in a while and pay special attention to her by reinforcing her basic obedience commands or having her perform one of her favorite tricks for treats.

On moving day, you have two options: taking Emma to a doggy day care, a kennel, or your veterinary clinic, if it offers boarding facilities, or keeping her in a closed room in your home. If Emma already likes doggy day care, this provides a perfect outlet for her to expend some energy with canine chums in a safe, supervised setting. When you pick her up at the end of the day, she will be tired and relaxed, even when walking into a near-empty house. Even if she is not used to being away from home, it might be less stressful for her to spend a few hours (or even a day or two) being cared for by professionals while you focus on the activity back at the house without having to worry about how Emma is doing.

If you do opt to keep her at home, choose a room that has already been cleared of all furnishings. Place a big sign on colored paper on the door to alert the movers that your dog is inside. During the hustle of moving items, you don't want to risk Emma escaping in fright and getting lost or hit by a car. If she likes her crate, let her stay in there with her favorite chew toy and water in a closed room. If she doesn't have a crate, provide her with her familiar bedding, a couple of favorite toys, a chew toy, and water. Turn on a portable radio to mute the sounds of the moving crew. Make sure she is wearing a collar and ID tags (or even better, a microchip ID).

It is very important that you take her for a 10-minute walk every few hours. Make sure you put her leash on before you leave the room. Encourage her to meet and greet the movers if they are willing. Speak in happy and calm tones. Dogs are masters at picking up our emotions.

Before you move into your new condo, see if your realtor is willing to place one of your used T-shirts or towels and a couple of Emma's saliva-slobbered toys inside the condo before you arrive. Just mail them in advance of your cross-country trek. That way, when Emma steps her first paw in your new place, she will immediately smell and see familiar objects to help her feel more at home.

Not the Right Dog for Our Family

Q We're in a dilemma. My wife and I adopted a two-year-old collie for our three children. They are now between the ages of nine and thirteen and have pestered us to get a dog for many years. They finally reached the ages where we felt they were mature enough to help with the responsibilities of having a dog. The problem is that Buster isn't fitting into our family. He barks constantly, chews the kid's toys, is hard to walk, and generally causes havoc in the house. We've taken him to obedience classes and worked with a behaviorist, but nothing has helped. What's worse, the dog doesn't seem to show much affection toward us, especially our kids. He does his best to avoid them. He is a real handful. We don't want to surrender him to a shelter, but this just isn't working out. Even our children don't want him any more. What are our options?

A Sometimes, despite all efforts, things do not work out with a particular dog. Even though you have made a concerted effort to make this situation work, this is a case of the wrong dog in the wrong household. It is telling that the dog does not appear to have bonded with any of you. Perhaps he feels overwhelmed by the number of people in the house.

Your first option is to contact Buster's breeder if you know who that is. A conscientious breeder will usually take back a dog who doesn't work out, or will at least help you find a new home. If you did not buy the dog from a breeder, I suggest that you contact a collie rescue group. You can find one in your area by checking the Internet for a national collie rescue organization or asking local collie breeders to put you in touch with a group in your area. Breed rescue groups, for the most part, do a wonderful job of matching the right dog with the right home.

Rescue groups are most successful when they are armed with detailed and accurate information. When you speak with the representative, be as specific and as honest as possible. List Buster's habits (good and bad) and the efforts you made to try to train him. Instead of staying in a cage at an animal shelter, Buster will probably be placed in a foster home with people who know the collie breed until a suitable permanent home can be found. It sounds as though he may fare better in a household without children or one in which there are definite daily routines for him to heed.

Don't automatically discount shelters, however. If there is one in your area, call and ask if they euthanize dogs and what the chances are of Buster being adopted. Even if you do not surrender him, the staff may be able to provide you with some good information.

Another option is to find a new home for Buster on your own. Although feasible, this can be time-consuming and frustrating. Plus, there are no guarantees or assurances that Buster will stay in home number two before being booted out to a third home, or worse, a shelter where he may face euthanasia.

> **SNIFF IT OUT!**
> Consumers spend $1.5 billion a year on pet food. That is four times the amount spent on baby food.

Still, it may be worth the effort to solicit the help of friends and relatives to alert others about the need to find Buster a better home. There may be someone out there who proves to be a better fit with Buster.

Whatever you do, please do not place a "free to a good home" ad in your local newspaper. You are just inviting people who are not serious about adopting a dog or making the financial commitment that pet ownership requires. They may neglect Buster or sell him to places that perform lab tests on dogs. Finally, do not be in a hurry. Yes, Buster is a handful, but you want to place him in a safe environment and one that will last.

GIVING UP THE DOG

Every year, millions of companion animals are surrendered to shelters around the country. A recent survey of shelters ranked these top ten reasons that people surrender their dogs.

Moving

Landlord issues

Cost of caring for a dog

No time for a dog

Inadequate facilities

Too many pets in the home

Dog is too sick

Personal problems

The dog bites

No homes found for litter

PROFESSIONAL CONSULTANTS

I was fortunate in having the assistance of three animal behavior experts in the writing of this book.

PATRICK MELESE is director of Veterinary Behavior Consultants in San Diego, a clinic that serves practitioners, clients, breeders, rescue groups, and institutions with specific companion animal behavior issues. A diplomate of the American College of Veterinary Behaviorists, Dr. Melese earned a master's degree in zoology and doctorate in veterinary medicine from the University of California in Davis. Visit his Web site, www.sdvetbehavior.com, for more information.

ALICE MOON-FANELLI is a certified applied animal behaviorist and clinical assistant professor at Cummings School of Veterinary Medicine at Tufts University, North Grafton, MA. She works in the Animal Behavior Center, which offers a remote consultation service (www.tufts.edu/vet/petfax). She received her doctorate and master degrees in etiology and canine behavior genetics from the University of Connecticut. An expert on dog and wolf behavior, Dr. Moon-Fanelli is a regular contributor to *Your Dog* and *Catnip* magazines.

PIA SILVANI, one of the country's top certified professional dog trainers, is director of training and behavior at St. Hubert's Animal Welfare Center in Madison, NJ (www.sthuberts.org). She is past vice president and charter member of the Association of Professional Dog Trainers. Ms. Silvani teaches everything from puppy socialization to Feisty Fido classes for dogs who need to control their tempers. She writes training manuals, lectures around the world, and is an advisor to the National Association of Professional Pet Sitters. Her first book, with co-author Lynn Eckhardt, is called *Raising Puppies & Kids Together: A Guide for Parents.*

SELECTED RESOURCES

American Humane Association, www.americanhumane.org

American Kennel Club, www.akc.org

American Society for the Prevention of Cruelty to Animals, www.aspca.org

American Veterinary Medical Association, www.avma.org

Delta Society, www.deltasociety.org

Humane Society of the United States, www.hsus.org

PetDiets.com, www.petdiets.com

ANIMAL BEHAVIOR

Animal Behavior Network, www.animalbehavior.net

International Association of Animal Behavior Consultants, www.iaabc.org

Association of Pet Dog Trainers, www.apdt.com

Clicker Training, www.clickertraining.com

LIVING WITH PETS

Dating web sites for people with pets.

www.animalattraction.com
www.animalpeople.com
www.datemypet.com

Sites to help you find pet-friendly housing.

www.apartmentguide.com
www.forrent.com
www.rentwithpets.com

Seek pet sitters in your area.

www.petsitter.org
www.petsit.com

Resources for traveling with your pets.

www.pets-allowed-hotels.com; www.travelingpets.com;
www.takeyourpet.com; www.pettravel.com; www.fidofriendly.com

TEMPORARY DOGS
If you are interested in training service puppies, start with these
organizations.

Canine Companions, www.caninecompanions.org
National Foundation for the Blind, www.nfb.org
Paws With a Cause, www.pawswithacause.org

LOSS OF A PET
Some organizations that can help you deal with the
death of a pet.

Association for Pet Loss & Bereavement, www.aplb.org

Rainbow Bridge, www.rainbowbridge.com

Tufts University Pet Loss Support Hotline
508-839-7966
www.tufts.edu/vet/petloss/

University of California-Davis, School of Veterinary Medicine
Pet Loss Support Hotline
800-565-1526
www.vetmed.ucdavis.edu/petloss/index.htm

RECOMMENDED READING

Adams, Janine. *How To Say It To Your Dog.* Prentice Hall Press, 2003.

Beck, Alan. *Between Pets and People: The Importance of Animal Companionship.* Purdue University Press, 1996.

Becker, Marty. *The Healing Power of Pets.* Hyperion, 2002.

Case, Linda P. *The Dog: Its Behavior, Nutrition & Health.* Iowa State University Press, 1999.

Choron, Sandra and Harry. *Planet Dog: A Doglopedia.* Houghton Mifflin, 2005.

Coren, Stanley. *The Intelligence of Dogs.* Free Press, 1994.

Dodman, Nicholas. *If Only They Could Speak: Stories about Pets and Their People.* Norton, 2002.

Fuhrman, Sue. *Canine Massage: A Balancing Act.* Wolfchase Press, 2000.

Hoffman, Matthew, ed. *Dog Speak.* Rodale, 1999.

Landsberg, Gary, Hunthausen, Wayne, and Ackerman, Lowell. *Handbook of Behavior Problems of the Dog and Cat.* Elsevier Saunders, 2003.

Pryor, Karen. *Don't Shoot the Dog: The New Art of Teaching and Training.* Bantam Books, 1999.

Sheldrake, Rupert. *Dogs That Know When Their Owners Are Coming Home and Other Unexplained Powers of Animals.* Three Rivers Press, 2000.

Silvani, Pia and Eckhardt, Lynn. *Raising Puppies & Kids Together: A Guide for Parents.* TFH Publications, 2006.

Yin, Sophia. *How To Behave So Your Dog Behaves.* TFH Publications, 2004.

INDEX

Page numbers in **bold** indicate tables.